MW01245126

MINIMALIST LIVING

Using Minimalism to Declutter Your Lifestyle - Habits & Mindsets to Live More & Worry Less!

JASON DELUCCI

TABLE OF CONTENTS

INTRODUCTION

Where It All Began

I was walking down my driveway one chilly February morning. It was 7:15 am, and my BMW 5 Series was sitting on the pavement as it always was. I opened the icy door, sat in the driver's seat and prepared myself for the hour commute in rush hour traffic. The office was in Baltimore, around 40 miles from where I lived in Rockville. I had intentionally moved out this way to bag a bigger apartment. It was a modern duplex close to a 2000 sq ft in size. More space for more stuff was the plan, even if it meant a 2 hour round trip to work each day.

For a time this all seemed fine. I justified the driving as a chance to wake up in the morning and wind down in the evening. It wasn't until I lost my job later that year did I see the craziness in all of this. It was 2008, and the financial crisis was in full swing. I worked for a premium textiles company in a high-level marketing position for several years up until this point. I did what my parents told me to do. I went to college, got a degree, then went to work for an established company in a stable job. I also did what everyone else does when an economy is going well. I leveraged my paycheck to the max with the biggest apartment and fastest car I could afford.

Everything was working great until it wasn't. My colleagues began to get laid off at an alarming rate, including myself. How was I going to pay my rent now? I'd just signed a new two year lease. How was I going to meet the finance requirements on my way too expensive German car?

The answer was I couldn't. It felt like a disaster, and even led to a full on breakdown accompanied by a couple of serious panic attacks. I'm not ashamed about this or afraid to admit it, as I now see this experience as a blessing. I had to look at things differently now. I was forced to take a new approach. Its been ten years almost to the day since those testing times. Its been a decade since I took on minimalism as a lifestyle, initially out of necessity, but now by choice.

All I can say is that I've never been happier and more content. I dare say we are due another significant financial correction, but I no longer fear the consequences. In truth, we are never more than a few years away from at least a typical recession. Unfortunately, when this does happen, a whole host of people will be subjected to the fears and pressures I suffered back in 2008. But it doesn't have to be this way, hence why I am writing this book. Whether you were forced to adopt this philosophy due to financial reasons or not, makes no difference. Its wise to start cutting down your clutter, to begin clearing the objects in your life and the worries in your mind. We have a finite amount of cognitive space to do our creative work in this world. Therefore its imperative to get rid of some stuff to allow this flourishing to happen.

Minimalism isn't a rejection of all material goods. It isn't a drastic austerity measure. It isn't a radical shift, but rather the continual act of streamlining and editing the things which are essential to you. Its a mindful way of living which gives precedent and focus to the present moment. To the things in our life right now, the way we are meant to live. This doesn't mean functioning with reckless abandon or without regard for your future self. Instead, well-executed minimalism requires careful planning and continual upkeep to remain on track. It just gets a lot easier with time, and well worth the shift when you do decide to make the change.

But how did we get to this point? Our conformity to a consumerist lifestyle in my opinion. We've all seen how this is portrayed and promulgated in the advertising world. TV commercials, music videos, and media of all forms promote conspicuous consumption. It drives us to buy that new car, watch or pair of shoes, just to keep up with the Joneses for another year. We buy on emotions but rationalize with logic after the fact. Companies know this and tap into these instincts within us. They know if they can get us to buy their products, we become familiar with their brand and feel a connection to it. We are then way more likely to be a repeat customer, and even do their bidding when it comes to promotion of the brand.

This is because we are social animals and continually looking to seek approval from the rest of the pack. We need to convey our value to the group, and there is no clearer way than flaunting our possessions. But the pleasure we derive from these purchases is always short lived. There is always the next iPhone being released just a few short months away. This is again why advertising works. It's not the product we want, but the lifestyle benefit the shiny new object provides us. Its the status symbols we are typically after. But these feelings fade away very quickly.

In my experience of running on the accumulation hamster wheel for more years than I'd like to admit, its a dead end. In fact, its worse than that. It's a sure fire way to unhappiness, while quickly becoming broke in the process. Once you have become accustomed and acclimatized to a certain standard of living, its hard to downsize in your mind, so you might as well skip the consumerism and go straight to the source that satisfies the human soul. Fill the hole in our being with only the things which bring us real joy. Focus on your personal qualities, not your possessions. It's not about being frugal for no reason, but rather tipping the balance towards that end of the spectrum for the sake of your sanity. When you do this in an intentional manner, its the most liberating feeling in the world.

A Fresh Approach

Like every psychological battle we face throughout life, the struggle is an internal one. Stress, worry and overwhelm is more prevalent in today's society than at any point in human history from what we can tell which is why this message resonates with so many when they find it. It takes a psychological separation of your identity from your possessions. It requires the undoing of much consumerist programming, from a bombardment of advertising exposure over the years. It requires a conscious effort to buck this accumulation trend and head in the opposite direction.

Think of the story of the mother & daughter at Thanksgiving. For years the daughter would watch her mom cut the ends off the ham before placing it in the oven. When it was her turn to entertain the family in later years, she instinctively did the same. But when the mother saw this, she was puzzled and asked: "why are you cutting the ends off the ham dear?" To which the daughter replied, "Because that's how you did it all these years." The mother laughed and replied, "That's because we had a smaller oven, and the ham wouldn't fit in the pan!". Do you ever question why you are doing what you are doing? Minimalism forces this contemplation upon us, it allows us to reassess what society has been telling us to do all along.

In essence, its a quality over quantity mentality, a priorities over possessions measure. It gives you the ability to reconnect with what's right. What's truly important in your life. Its a trade off from physically owning stuff, for mental clarity and freedom in your thinking. Everything you own comes at a cost. Typically monetary and logistically at first, but then in a cognitive real estate sense later down the line. You have to allocate space to thinking about it on a frequent basis. This might not sound like a lot, but start to add up all of your belongings, and it quickly becomes an avalanche of contemplation. You don't just store things in your cupboards; you have to file them in your head too.

You have to make the choice that you are going to do this and be comfortable with it. You have to permit yourself to let go of things and know that you will be OK once they are gone. You will make the odd mistake at first, wish you had kept something you gave away perhaps. But quickly realize that nobody dies when you couldn't get it back. It's a little like a relationship breakup. It seems impossible on the first attempt. But after some time working through the outcomes, the path becomes clear. There will be some discomfort as with all new beginnings. But ultimately it's for the best.

So I aim to take you down this road, to show you the possibilities of a new liberating existence. Although I have a slightly different take on minimalism in general. Yes, I want to cut down the noise in my life, but I still want to be successful. For me, downsizing everything just won't do. I have indeed cut out the clutter in my life, but more from choice than absolute necessity. I still want a beautiful house, just not to fill it with useless stuff. I still want a nice car, but only one.

But most importantly of all, I want to instill in you the proper clarity of thought principles, which are so critical for a harmonious life. Thus this first installment in the minimalism series is dedicated to mindset more than anything. Thinking in a streamlined manner is the starting point to success with this philosophy. The methods I've laid out are simple but not easy. They will require some work but if you are willing to put in a little effort up front, it's impossible not to reap the benefit from them. So let's not ponder these upsides any longer, let me show you how to achieve them!

CHAPTER 1: MINIMALISM MYTHS & MISCONCEPTIONS

"Minimalism is about intentionality, not deprivation."

(Dejan Stojanivic)

Before we get into the nitty-gritty of genuine minimalist living, it's important to define precisely what minimalism is. This philosophy was conceptualized by the visual arts movement in the 1960's. It was conceived by a number of prominent New York artists at the time, who took a reductionist approach to modernism. In practice, it was the act of stripping away anything that was superfluous to the piece, leaving only the essential. I'm no art bod, but this seemed like a revolutionary move at the time to those who would spend their weekends staring at art gallery walls.

However, this mindset quickly found its way into the prevailing culture, especially with regards to how people were arranging their living space. The act of decluttering the house or apartment became trendy and has continued to gain popularity until today. This is the reason why I've dedicated an entire edition in this series to the specifics of a minimalist home. If you haven't checked that one out yet, I recommend taking a look. It may be available for pre-order or perhaps general sale depending on when you read this. I began to write all three books as one initially, although I quickly realized that the advice was heavily compartmentalized into three distinct categories, I.e., Mindset, the home, and in a financial sense. Hence the three books.

Therefore this first edition primarily focuses on the general life principles of the "less is more" philosophy, and for good reason. If you can get your head aligned correctly, to begin with, a minimalist mindset can then be successfully applied to any area you wish. In this sense, I find it best to get your daily tasks, habits, and interactions in line first and foremost, as they have the biggest payoff over time. Yes, your home is important too, as its the place everyone naturally wants to start. It's the most natural area to apply the notions of minimalism as there is solid stuff to throw away.

But your living space is only part of the puzzle. Unless you are a stay at home parent or have a home office, you will likely spend the majority of your time in the wild so to speak. You will be commuting to and from work, interacting with friends and colleagues, at the gym and traveling for vacations. But most importantly of all, you will be spending all of this time between your own two ears! This is why I focus on the psychological principles of this lifestyle so much, and not just the organizational strategies to implement it.

So before we get into discussing what these particulars are with regards to putting minimalism into practice, and successfully within your own life. It's wise to point out some of the major myths about this philosophy before doing so. To dispel some of the main misconceptions in order to truly understand it for yourself. I've touched upon a few of these already, but the following are some of the main pitfalls and resistances I've come across when it comes to embodying the minimalist lifestyle over the years:

1. Minimalists have to do without modern conveniences

On the contrary, advanced technology makes minimalism easier to achieve in my opinion (more on this later). You certainly do not have to forego modern appliances to survive with this philosophy by any stretch of the imagination. As always, it's about retaining what's important and essential to you. It requires you to assess the use of something, not merely obsessing over its vintage. Whether that's a smart kitchen appliance to help streamline your culinary activities, or a piece of digital tech to help organize and store your documents. Modern amenities should be embraced, not shunned.

2. You have to live in a tiny house

I get into this in much greater detail within the second edition to this series. But living off the grid in a micro-apartment isn't necessary either. Remember that true minimalism isn't about less space, but rather what you do with it. It's not about living in a small house, but what you decide to fit into the space you do have. This is where most people get confused. They want to downsize their home to reduce its upkeep. You see this all the time with retirees. They do not want the hassle of excessive maintenance a large house requires. But again, it's not the space which is the issue, but the stuff which needs managing within it.

I'm a testament to this. I now live in a reasonably sized apartment with ample square footage. There is more than enough clear space to make my sparsely, but well-placed furniture pop. If anything, a smaller unit can make minimalism more challenging to achieve concerning your physical possessions, depending on your storage capabilities. So hold off on instructing your realtor to find you that newer cozier place for now. Let's work on streamlining your current abode, to begin with.

3. You can only own a set amount of things, I.e., 100 objects

A minimalist mindset is more about simplicity, not a one size fits all, rigid framework approach. A better strategy for most people is halving the number of possessions they own as a general rule of thumb. So what you are ultimately left with will depend on your starting point. The other myth is that you have to know exactly what you own at all times. This is again overkill in my eyes, and takes up much-unwanted space in your head, just by making these calculations. Minimalism, when done correctly, is an intuitive exercise, you can see and feel what is too much or what is just about right. Don't over think this; it defies the point entirely when you do.

A simple approach applies to all areas of life, not merely possessions. It's not about cataloging everything you own and over complicating the process. That defeats the point of minimalism in the first place. That sounds like too much effort for me. I got into this as I wanted to cut down the mental work I needed to do regarding menial tasks. It's simply about cutting out what you don't need, starting with the low hanging fruit, then optimizing as you go.

4. You have to go without

Following on from the modern conveniences point, a minimalist doesn't give up what is important and useful to them just for the sake of it. They only become good at eradicating what isn't. They give up what isn't necessary for their life for what is. Its the ultimate FOMO (Fear Of Missing Out) countermeasure. When you genuinely assess what gives you the most enjoyment and return of investment of your time, it's far easier to let the inconsequential stuff go.

When I choose not to purchase that new toy or turn down the opportunity to socialize with friends, I think to myself "what am I actually missing here?" Once you get over that initial feeling of loss, you will instantly feel better I can assure you. You quickly return to the stable state of mind this philosophy encourages. You will often hear the somewhat overused and clichéd statement that "you were born with nothing, and you'll leave this life with nothing too", but this is eminently true. I'm not saying don't accumulate any of the trappings that material wealth can provide, minimalism isn't about going without. Just get good at deciding what you really want, and just get that instead!

5. Minimalists only wear monochrome clothes

If there is one question I get asked most often regarding this lifestyle, its how many clothes I own. This is why I have dedicated an entire chapter to the considerations of your wardrobe within *"Minimalist Home."* People immediately assume I only have one pair of underwear for each day of the week (OK this is true). But it doesn't mean my clothes are lifeless and dull. I am now forced to choose precisely what I like to wear in each instance. I select that one winter coat I love, that perfect pair of formal shoes, that awesome trucker cap. Yes, I arrange my cupboard in terms of color, but I assure you there's plenty of it.

There's a misconception that minimalists are a boring bunch who continuously want to suck the fun out of life. But on the contrary, these folks are some of the most interesting and eccentric people I know. We are just more selective with our possessions, and that certainly pertains to what we choose to wear.

6. Minimalists are always single.

I won't lie, its easier to initially adopt this lifestyle if you only have yourself to worry about. When you just have your own things to sort out. However, there's a great benefit to being a minimalist couple or family. Kids have truckloads of stuff. Toys pile up into Everest style mountains on their bedroom floor if you're not careful. But just like yourself, it's not about making them go without, but instead simply instilling better values within them. Kids don't do what their parents tell them; they do what they see them doing. So be the example to follow. Remember it's going to take a generation at least to break the cycle of endless consumerism, so you might as well get started now.

I will say that once you get your partner on board, things can become even more streamlined than ever. I'm lucky in that sense. Back when I started on this minimalism mission, my girlfriend at the time (now my wife) was fully on-board with it. In reality, I'm not sure what we would have done if she wasn't. It doesn't mean you can't be with someone if they don't share the same values as you in this sense. I'm not evangelical in my ways. It's just that much easier if your living partner is of the same mind. There's much less friction when it comes to arranging the house, in addition to making social and travel plans too. I had an idea of creating a dating app to help other minimalists find the perfect partner! Maybe I'll get to that after I've published these books.

7. Minimalism is only about objects and things.

In my view, this is the most critical misconception of all. As I've mentioned, this way of doing things is predominantly a psychological pursuit. Letting go of mental baggage which hinders your life is paramount to achieving harmony and peace of mind. It's about freedom more than anything, and the ability to let things go. Releasing the hangups we have about the past, and preventing endless postulation about the future. Henry Ford once stated that "Thinking is the hardest work there is, which is probably why so few people do it." I wouldn't disagree with this. That is why I want to help you streamline your thinking if I can.

I have some very actionable advice in this regard — some sage concepts that we will explore in much greater detail within the paragraphs to follow. I'm big on getting the mind in shape first and foremost. In a holistic and non-dualistic sense, nothing can truly be separated anyway. We are conscious beings who have to navigate this physical world by interacting with it, whether that's the thoughts in our heads or our physical actions. It takes both a rational and emotional effort to perform. Minimalism is just about identifying where best to direct this attention.

So now that we know what we are dealing with and what we need to be aiming for when striving for minimalist living. Let's dive in and take a look at the specific area's in which we can cut down the clutter in our lives. I promise you; it will be well worth the time and effort you will put into this.

CHAPTER 2: RELATIONSHIPS - FAMILY, FRIENDS & CO-WORKERS

"Paying attention to the people you love is 2% effort, and 98% not looking at your phone."

(Anonymous)

I honestly think this can be the most crucial area to get leverage on yourself, which is why I have chosen to start here. That's because humans are emotional creatures by very nature. We are affected dramatically by those around us, especially our significant others. Close friends and family have such a big impact on our mental state if we let them. Even colleagues and co-workers to some extent, due to the lengths of time we spend in their presence throughout the day. This is why it's critical to correctly apply the rules of minimalism towards the relationships and interactions you have.

Maximizing Relationships ROI

Minimalism forces you to really decide what you like doing, what is giving you the highest ROI (Return On Investment) of your time. If hanging out at that same old bar only gives you a hangover and lighter wallet, then stop doing it. If continually associating with negative people is bringing you down, then start to cut them out of your life. Its said that you will become the aggregate of the five people you most commonly spend time with. Or show me your friends and I'll show you your future. If this is true, which it largely is from what I can tell, then you really have to assess who these people are in your own life.

This will be easier with regards to acquaintances and work colleagues, but less so concerning close friends and family for obvious reasons. These individuals have a much closer emotional bond with us, and its natural to want to appease them when they request our time and attention. My Advice is simply to do the best you can, try to reduce your exposure to that difficult sibling or crazy aunt. This is where geography can be your friend. If you can put enough space between yourself and them, it's much more difficult to get drawn into every silly drama they instigate.

But as a general rule, try to spend time with those who give you net positive benefits. This isn't being selfish. Your mental health is paramount. You can't love those around you if you don't love yourself first. You can't contribute in a positive manner if you are always fighting to get out of a negative state. You will feel guilty about this to begin with, which is normal. So I give you permission to start this cull if you need it.

This will typically be easier for natural introverts like myself. I found that I never enjoyed going to social events and work gatherings if truth be told. I struggled with the endless pleasantries and small talk. I'm not saying you shouldn't network when needed, or be impolite to those you come across. But don't feel that you need to be the social butterfly either. Hobnobbing with these groups ad infinitum is a road to unhappiness in my experience. Remember that friends should be a very select bunch you choose to allocate time to. The interactions and conversations you will have will be that much more profound and enriching as a result.

But first, we need a strategy to identify the areas of issue. To pinpoint those who are causing you the most problems from a time and energy standpoint. This is where you will make the most headway of all. Once more, this isn't an unemphatic dig at these people. Everyone is going through their own version of this game we call life. I don't judge anyone too harshly for their actions, as I've never walked in their shoes. But I don't condone continual lousy behavior. I just see these instances as unconscious acts for the most part. I know that these folks will one day look back on these situations with regret. I certainly wish I had acted differently on occasions myself. So I just do my best to help others where I can, but it's not my (or your) responsibility to continually handhold them along this journey.

Dealing With Energy Vampires

In reality, It should be quite clear who these people are in your life. Most of you will intuitively know them, even if you do not want to call it how it is out loud. Whether you wish to label them or not, these are the individuals you know you have to cut down your exposure to. Retaining frequent communication with such a person, whether that be a friendship or romantic relationship, can become an exhausting exercise. It quickly becomes the very antithesis of living a minimalist lifestyle, where conserving energy for the important things is a priority. Energy vampires are known for feeding off negative attention. They are often extraordinarily deceptive and manipulative. Just being around these individuals can drain you emotionally, so be wary of anyone exhibiting the following traits:

- Extreme Paranoia

- Substantial egoic nature, leading to disagreements and arguments

- A propensity to become passive-aggressive

- Melodramatic tendencies

- Narcissistic attitude

- A tendency to gossip around you

- Extreme insecurity

- Highly jealous behavior

I once had a friend back in college who displayed many of these attributes in spades. When looking back on the situation, it was clear that we weren't really friends at all. It was a one way street in terms of attention, I.e., everything flowing to him. At the time I just viewed the guy as unfortunate. He came from a less than privileged background, and while having almost all of his tuition and accommodation supplemented by the school, he still hardly lifted a finger to make the experience work in his favor.

I would frequently find myself buying us lunch, helping with his coursework while simultaneously providing an ear to any girl trouble he had. I think I felt bad because my father had helped me so much with my own financial position, that I was trying to compensate in some way by giving so much time and attention away. But one day it dawned on me that I'd done enough. Both of my parents had worked darn hard in their lives to afford me this opportunity, and I was blowing it. I owed it to them as well as myself to graduate with honors and be able to pay them back in the future. Once this was clear, I cut almost all ties with this not so fruitful friendship, which was a massive burden off my shoulders. In fact, I did the guy a huge favor in doing so. Even though he tried the same tactics on others within our group initially, he eventually realized the error of his ways and started to take on much more responsibility in the latter years of knowing him.

So once you have determined those who exhibit these symptoms on a consistent basis in your own life, it's time to start deploying a minimalist strategy to reduce the adverse effects they have over you. This doesn't just mean cutting down the time you spend with them, but also conserving and protecting your energy in the moments when you do see them. Otherwise, it's easy to become overwhelmed, stressed, physically or mentally exhausted, anxious, and irritable if you're not careful. Set clear boundaries with these people. Avoid reacting to their tendencies when you can. Stick to light topics, but most importantly, learn to say NO more.

While it's undoubtedly difficult to deal with narcissists and energy vampires, especially if they're members of your close friends or family group, you can still do so with proper practice and implementation of these strategies. The biggest one for me is learning to turn people down for requests of my time. To alleviate me from the guilt of not picking up the phone or responding to every message. I have some minimalist friends who have employed some rather extreme measures to do this. A common practice is to simply change your cell phone number. One guy I know even recorded a voicemail message saying "I have changed my number, if I haven't given you the new one, then you are no longer a part of my life!". Its entirely up to you if you want to go this far, I wouldn't have to heart to do it myself. But I do encourage you to take some tangible steps in this direction, in addition to heeding the following advice.

Improving Your Inner Circle

This should also be reasonably obvious information, but most people still do not take as much notice of this concept as they should. If you are implementing the previous methods of eradicating problematic people, then this will come as a natural consequence anyway. If you are no longer associating with those who do not have your best interests at heart, you will be left with only the gems. You will now be around positive and high-performance people by default, those who are willing to support you and raise your standards. Once more, this is easier said than done with regards to close friends and family, but you do have to draw the line somewhere. Be with people who provide genuine positive upsides to your life.

Make a conscious effort to socialize with those who encourage your progress and feed your confidence. Enact the base principles of minimalism to those you associate with most often. Really take inventory of these people. This is the area I see folks struggle with most, due to the connections and emotions they feel within their existing relationships. But I'll make no apologies for stressing it again; this is where the most progress can be made. Good relationships of all kinds should be a mutually beneficial communion. The whole should be greater than the sum of the parts when all is said and done.

There are many social studies which indicate that humans live longer the happier they are. This also occurs in regions with strong community bonds such as rural Mediterranean villages, or the Japanese island of Okinawa which is famous for the longevity of its inhabitants. Much of this has to do with diet (more on this later), but much can also be attributed to the communal nature of these people. Everyone you come across is considered family in these places, and they help each other out accordingly. Minimalism just aids with the process considerably. The fewer things you own, the more time you have to engage in deep conversations with those who you have chosen to keep around. I certainly appreciate my wife that much more now. We seldom fight, if ever now that we are free to talk through any situation before it becomes a problem.

So get busy building this tight-knit community of your own. Eradicate the negative individuals from your circle, and you'll find you are much happier and at ease when you do. Becoming ruthless with your time is critical, as its the most important commodity of all. We can get our possessions back if we lose them, but the same can't be said for your time. If you need some further tips on how to manage and protect yours more efficiently, then the following chapter will show you how.

CHAPTER 3: TIME, TASKS & PROJECTS

"NO is a complete sentence"

(Anne Lamott)

You will often hear people say that you should manage your time wisely. What they are really saying is manage your energy more efficiently. That's because time is undoubtedly finite, but so is the life juice within you. If you have lots of it, you can fit more into the time you do have, and you can utilize it to a far greater extent. It's just a matter of priorities, and what you choose to focus on. If you require a long time to recharge your batteries, then you'll need to manage your activities accordingly. As I've already mentioned, it's OK to say no to social events and "catch-ups" with friends in this sense.

I certainly struggled with this at first. I could never say no to things. But the magic happens when you do, and realize that it's not the end of the world. You don't lose friends overnight. They actually respect you more if you aren't so liberal with your time. This isn't being self-centered. Remember that self-care is your duty, which requires careful management of your activities. You should find this becomes easier with age, but everyone should intentionally cultivate this trait whatever stage of life you are at. It's essential for improving the quality of the fewer interactions you do have.

So how do we maximize the activities which are left? Clearing your schedule is one thing, but if you haven't planned how you are now going to fill your day, you may end up staring at the wall instead. To aid with this, you'll need some methods to help optimize your time and energy — some ways to produce above-average results, without spending every waking hour working on these tasks. We are minimalists after all, so efficiency is always the name of the game. Everyone has read or at least heard of *"The 4-Hour Work Week"* by Tim Ferriss. Some view his ideas as the starting point for modern-day minimalism as the concepts he focuses on within his excellent book, describe some of the practical measures to implement this philosophy well. Such advice includes valuing your time, freedom and ability to travel and work where you wish. There's a linear theme to creating this lifestyle which requires the elimination of the unimportant, streamlining and simplifying what's left, and also automating what you can.

I struggle to improve on this stellar advice. However, I have honed some strategies that have personally worked great for me over the years. So the following are methods I have distilled down from my own experience. I know they will be beneficial to others too if you put them into practice yourself.

Productivity Hacking

Minimalism merely is about adjusting your thinking patterns before implementing positive habits and behavioral traits to help the mindset take hold. This relates to all of the tasks and projects we take on, as well as the time we allocate to them. I have found a productivity principle to help you along the way if you are struggling with managing tasks. Its a technique I use myself, to be more efficient. The idea is simply to set out to do a manageable amount of work each day and do it EVERYDAY. It's one of the most potent minimalist hacks when performed over the long run.

When you aggregate these small workloads together, they really start to add up. I use this strategy when writing new material. I don't try to finish a book within a month or write 5000 words in a day. That only leads to burn out and lower quality work. But rather, I ensure that I produce only 1000 high-quality words instead. I'll take Sunday off to clear my head, but that's OK. Writing 1000 words, six days a week for a year is plenty. Even if I take a two week holiday, that still amounts to 300,000 words per year — something which seems unachievable at first, but eminently possible when employing this technique. This principle works the same when growing and compounding your finances, but that's a discussion for another day.

In fact, it works with just about every endeavor you can think of, work, exercise, finances, etc. Performing a moderate amount of high-quality activity each day always comes out ahead. People intuitively equate doing less with being lazy. But Rome wasn't built in a day as they say. You don't set out to build a wall. Instead, you decide to lay one brick perfectly at a time. Focus on doing that each day, and soon enough you'll have your skyscraper. It's about focused and deliberate action which counts. Practice doesn't make perfect. Perfect practice makes perfect. Repetition of sub-par work won't do the job. More on how to do this within visualization and goal setting next.

But in general, the trick is to live in one-day increments. To compartmentalize your life into 24 hour minimalist time frames. This ensures you only deal with tasks and projects as they arise. Dr. James Gilkey described this method in his 1944 sermon titled "Gaining Emotional Poise." He discovered the idea while gazing at an egg timer on his desk one afternoon. He noticed that the sand would pass from the top of the hourglass to the bottom in less than 10 minutes, albeit still only one grain at a time. Our lives are no different in this respect. Our problems line up in single file, and we deal with them one-by-one. But we act as though we need to solve every potential issue and cram all future tasks into the here and now.

If you can manage to change your thinking and working habits in this way, I.e., by taking things more slowly, but much more consistently, you will be well on your way to greater progress in anything you are attempting to do. Your productivity will increase, but you will feel like you are doing less. You are now able to achieve any worthwhile project as you have the proper game plan to do it. It's about consistent and directed effort and leaving yourself enough in the tank to do the same tomorrow. It has been shown that humans function best, and are most happy when we are performing structured and positive routines. We can more easily assess the changes and tweaks we make to our behaviors too, as they can be judged against our normal results. Anything which produces positive effects can then be integrated into our activities, while disregarding anything which didn't work.

That being said, there are some additional tips you can implement in order to form better minimalism habits. I dislike referring to psychological tools as "tips" or "secrets," as it suggests they are somehow shortcuts to success. This is the wrong way of looking at them. Yes, they can help you greatly if you are willing to put in the work. But everything requires some level of effort to implement, even as a minimalist. The trade-off is usually a sizable amount of work upfront, for a more comfortable life down the road. So the following are some of these additional techniques which should help you achieve this.

Priority Planning

The first of which is to deal with tasks that require your immediate attention first. If you are not working on a long-term project, like writing 300,000 words per year, then its easy to become distracted by any number of things throughout the day. Therefore, good old-fashioned planning is your friend here. You need to identify exactly what these activities are to begin with. If you need to clear your inbox of any critical correspondence before starting your day, then do so first thing without delay. Schedule 30 minutes to respond to these after breakfast for instance.

Pushing high priority work to later in the day will reduce its value, along with the likelihood it will get done. This seems like common sense, but I'm amazed at how many people can't put this simple productivity habit into practice each day. It's a good idea to identify and categorize all daily tasks in terms of what needs to be completed. Starting from the most critical, all the way down to the optional, then checking them off accordingly as you go.

It's the classic 80/20 rule in action, something which Ferriss highlights too. If there is one concept, a minimalist needs to assimilate its this. Most of your results, I.e., 80%, will come from the few, but essential actions, I.e., 20%. If you can identify what these high payoff activities are, you can focus solely on them, reducing your time and effort while still reaping excellent results. I outsource anything which doesn't fall into my 20% remit of tasks. For me that is everything other than writing. I could learn how to be a copywriter, build marketing funnels and graphic design book covers. But that's not my interest or area of expertise. I let other and more skilled people take care of that stuff for me. Delegation is incredibly liberating when you get it right. Perfectionists can struggle with this of course, I know I did for many years. But at some point you understand that you can't control every minute detail in life, and its not necessary to if you want to be successful. If you're doing things to the best of your ability every day, you'll be just fine. Set some deadlines as at some point you just have to say that "good enough, is good enough." Put a bow on it and get it out the door.

Multitasking Mistakes

This is especially pertinent advice for men, but women could also do well to heed this message too. Multitasking is never a good idea as it reduces your focus on the task at hand, which ultimately decreases productivity for the most part. Pay attention to just one activity at a time, and avoid the temptation to take on too many things at once. People presume they are being more efficient by being busy. But as we have seen already, this is a myth, and actually reduces productivity overall.

Remember that tasks are meant to be checked off one-by-one and in order of importance. Once you have planned out this activity effectively, your job is to simply get your head down and work through them. Take each day as it comes and don't worry unduly about subsequent tasks. They will also get completed in time, just like each grain of sand which passes through the egg timer without issue. I promise you, by doing things correctly from the outset, you will avoid any feelings of overwhelm by implementing this minimalistic working mindset.

A big help with this is eradicating distractions from your working space. Or only having positive things around which stimulate a productive response within you. That picture of your scaling Mount Kilimanjaro last year. Your favorite self-help book, that intercollegiate rowing medal you won. You get the idea. Instead of distracting, these visual cues encourage creative spontaneity. They help the subconscious mind do its best work. You clear the creative centers, as you are not clogging up the cognitive machinery with excessive worry and doubt, just positive input instead.

These principles work great if you happen to run your own business, as you are in full control of your time and activities. I'm not sure about 4 hours a week, but 4 hours a day is typically all you need. Crank these out in the morning when you are the most alert, and you should produce some of your most creative and productive work. But these factors also function great when implemented into a 9-5 where you have at least some level of autonomy. I used to think I was being productive by simply sitting in the office for 8 hours a day. In reality, I was logging into social media, making multiple cups of coffee and distracting myself with pointless meetings at every opportunity.

Heck, these concepts even apply to the retired grandparents who want to optimize their gardening work and time within the family better. As always this philosophy isn't about sucking the fun out of life, it's about putting more fun into the life that you do have. It's about enjoying the activities you do choose to indulge in, to appreciate all of life's currencies, not just money. It's about being as productive as possible with regards to the work you choose to take on. If you want some strategies to help you achieve this even more efficiently, then read on...

CHAPTER 4: VISUALIZE & GOAL SET THE PERFECT LIFE

"Minimalism is not a lack of something. It's simply the perfect amount of something."

(Nicholas Burroughs)

You can't do anything without first painting the picture of it in your mind. This is especially true when visualizing your perfect living space. However, it's equally relevant for anything you are trying to achieve in life. This is not some esoteric law of attraction advice. I'm not asking you to sit in a quiet corner until you manifest your dreams into existence. What I'm suggesting is a legitimate strategy to employ, especially for a minimalist. People tend to bumble through life bouncing from one instance to the next. You don't need me to highlight just how inefficient this is though. Its far better to ensure you direct your life more deliberately, to put yourself at the causal end of your environment, not always being subjected merely to its effects.

You want to be the conductor, which takes some conscious effort, to begin with. It requires some visualization and goal setting strategies to ensure you are heading in the right direction, as well as staying on track. It should make your life that much more streamlined when done correctly. Very few people take the time to plan out their future intentionally. This seems crazy to me, why would you let something as important as your existence on this planet be left to chance? But once again, this sounds like too much work for most people, which is why they don't do it.

It should be clear by now that I'm also not a fan of unguided effort, or just doing things for the sake of it. I'm a minimalist after all. I am all for efficiency though. Doing the necessary work to get what I want complete, but no more. This is why I employ the following two techniques when it comes to the important things in my day-to-day life. Yes, this will take a little work up front, but the payoff will be well worth it in the long run. What you will re-coup in terms of results will be substantial. So don't dismiss these without giving them a proper go for yourself.

Visualization - The Right Way

The first of these techniques requires some high-level mental imagery work. Almost everyone gets this wrong when it comes to getting what they want. People believe that the desires they have for themselves should be extremely specific, I.e., a particular house, specific holiday destination or an exact amount of money. They also want it in a definite time-frame, I.e., in 5 months or by some predetermined date. But if (or more like when) they fail to achieve this goal, they become disheartened and stop working on it altogether. They were told this by some well-intentioned but misinformed "life coach" who hasn't achieved anything of note themselves. But this way of thinking hardly ever works in practice.

Because its bad advice to begin with. I never set deadlines for the broader goals I'm striving for in life. Let me explain why. The human brain simply does not work in specifics regarding these achievements. The subconscious mind, which is ultimately responsible for actualizing these milestones, functions better with imagery, feelings, and emotions. It requires a different approach to the SMART goals we've all been conditioned to use, I.e. (Specific, Measurable, Attainable, Relevant & Time Based). In my experience, it takes another strategy. What we need is the correct use of visualization.

Purpose driven life goals should be grandiose, they should be hyper-ambitious. Think of it like aiming for the horizon line, which is impossible to reach in reality, as its a theoretical point. A far better strategy for longer-term goals is to create a picture or movie in your mind about what these things would look like. How do you envisage yourself once you have achieved these aspirations? What clothes are you wearing? How are you carrying yourself? What does your general demeanor now indicate about you?

The mind cannot differentiate between past, present and future events with regards to imagery in the mind. The body elicits the same biochemical response as if that experience was happening right now, especially when adequate emotion is applied. It's a clever trick which can convince the mind into believing that you have already achieved these things. The subconscious will then go to work in serving up additional and similar opportunities to bring into your physical reality.

"But Jason, isn't this just daydreaming?" you might ask. If you are not genuinely feeling the emotions attached to these images and have no intention of acting upon them, then yes it is. If however you truly believe that this image is where you are heading, or better yet, that you have already attained it, then it's visualization. Although its only part of the puzzle. Mental imagery can work wonders, but to ensure you are making some tangible progress towards these wants and desires, you need one more complementary strategy. You need to be able to goal set correctly, especially with regards to checking off short-term targets on the way to these achievements.

Goal Setting For Success

As we have already seen, long-term goals require subconscious guidance by and large, but we need a way to gauge short-term progress as well. This is where specific goals come into use. This type of thinking requires conscious forebrain activity, as the mind can conceive of tasks very precisely within a 1-3 month time period. It can vividly devise a plan for A to B activities without confusion. These are the objective KPI style metrics you may encounter in a corporate office job perhaps. You might need to achieve certain benchmarks each day, week or month to ensure productivity levels are satisfied, much like the consistent and directed effort we've already talked about in the previous chapter.

Have you ever wondered why it's challenging to lose weight for no real reason? But if you have to fit into that ball gown in 5 weeks time, then all of a sudden it becomes that much easier. The reason is that the mind has a definite target to aim at and a hard-coded time-frame by which to achieve it. This strategy works really well for anything within a 90-day time period. I.e., getting in condition to run a marathon or practicing for a driving test. The mind can see the goal clearly and knows what must be done to achieve it. But more importantly, it can see the finish line and envisage the steps required to get you there. Motivation becomes less of an issue as these set in stone deadlines propel a person to take action in anticipation of failure if they do not.

Focusing on the Few

But what should these goals be? What is the best strategy for a minimalist to follow? How can we squeeze the most out of our time and effort in a visualization and goal setting sense? How do we cut down the noise and zero in on only the critical? The strategy I use is one I've followed for years now, as it compliments a minimalist lifestyle perfectly. I'm not going to take credit for it, as I didn't invent it. It comes from an anecdotal story regarding Warren Buffett and his private jet pilot.

One day Warren asked the pilot why he hadn't achieved the goals he was striving for yet. He had been exposed to many of Buffet's dealings over the years and had more than enough experience and guidance simply by spending so much time in the expert investors presence. On reflection and after some discussion, they both agreed that it only boiled down to one thing which was his focus, or a lack thereof it.

Buffet asked the guy to note down the top 20 aspirations he had for himself. Then to rank them in order of priority, with 100% being the most important, all the way down to 50% being "nice to haves." So the pilot did this and excitedly returned them to his mentor the following day. Buffett took out a pen and crossed through everything on the list which didn't have 100% marked next to it. He circled the three remaining goals at the top of the page and gave it back stating "Here, just do these and only these for the next 20 years".

You don't have to be a super successful finance person or budding investor to heed this advice. But much can be gleaned from a guy who has amassed many billions of dollars by sticking to this principle. Buffett is famed for stating that he never does anything outside his scope of expertise and knowledge. He only focuses on what's important to him, and where he knows he can most predictably produce results. We can all use this advice when planning our own goals and efforts towards them.

If you want some examples of what this might look like, I have listed down 10 of my top 20 aspirations to give you an idea. I wrote these back in 2008 when I was first embarking on my minimalism journey. These are only meant to be a guide, they will likely be different for you, but hopefully will provide some inspiration to get you started. So don't delay in getting yours down on paper too:

Jason's Goals

100% - Become financially independent to provide for my family and me.

100% - Successfully implement minimalist strategies in all areas of my life.

100% -Write three books on how I achieved this so others can do the same.

95% - Buy my dream house with a lake view.

92% - Purchase an Aston Martin DB9.

90% - Learn to fly an airplane.

87% - Skydive over the Palm Islands in Dubai.

85 % - Volunteer for an NGO in Africa for six months.

83% - Run a Marathon in a sub-4-hour time.

78% - Learn to speak Spanish fluently.

You get the picture.

What you will find is the top 3 things you have written, should be purpose driven goals. They should be the things which are so critical, that life would not be worth living without achieving them. If you focus on visualizing and setting up short-term targets to reach them, then you will start to make immense progress in no time. What you should find is that you begin checking off many others down the list too, simply as a consequence of achieving the top 3. Becoming financially independent has allowed me to acquire many of the material and experiential things I listed down the line.

Again, for you, these might be similar or completely different, but that's not the point. The important thing is to physically write them down for yourself. Then you have a clear starting point and a game plan by which to work towards. Focus on the few, not the many, should be a minimalists battle cry. This advice applies to everything in life, such as attaining a better job, winning a sporting championship or merely creating a life of minimalism for yourself. But its especially relevant when it comes to the high-level goals you wish to achieve along the way.

CHAPTER 5: COMMUNICATION & TECHNOLOGY

"I've learned that minimalism isn't about what you own,
it's about why you own it."

(Brian Gardner)

There's never been a point in time when humans were freer to do what we like as we are today. Modern technology allows us to not only communicate with the rest of the world instantaneously but also to travel where we wish at the drop of a hat. As Peter Diamandis, the co-author of the book *"Abundance"* points outs. A Maasai Warrior with a smartphone today has better mobile communication than President Clinton did just 20 years ago. While these advancements are undoubtedly exciting, for the most part, they don't come without some significant downsides. If you often feel overwhelmed by all of this, then you're not alone. But if you know how to handle these factors properly, you can attain considerable leverage on yourself and prosper.

The traditional minimalism advice is to cut down your exposure to modern technology. To get rid of the laptop, iPad, computer and phone, or just make do with one. This is where I buck the trend a little. I'm a modern day minimalist in this sense. I see the benefits of our current tech when used responsibly and correctly of course. But that's the key, using these things optimally, and to simplify your life, not inundate it with yet more distractions. The following are some of the most effective strategies I've come across to help you do this.

Consolidate Electronics

There's no doubt that our digital tech is a double-edged sword. The ease of connectivity at our fingertips seems like a Godsend. However, the addictive nature of this instant gratification communication is real. We end up craving the reactions to our posts in the forms of likes, comments, and shares. Facebook uses a specific shade of red for its notification symbols, which has been scientifically tested to trigger attention-grabbing and action-provoking responses from within us. We simply HAVE to click on the icons to see what we are missing out on.

Similarly, the guy who designed the current news feed did so in line with Vegas-style slot machines. Swiping down on your phones LCD screen places random new posts at the top of the feed from friends and liked pages, as opposed to the original chronologically displayed versions of the past. While the posts are always relevant, we still do not know what they will be, hence the anticipation and excitement. It produces a dopamine hit each time we "spin the wheel." I personally do not spend any time scrolling through this feature anymore, due to its excessive time wasting and addictive nature. I'd highly recommend you do the same.

As contrary to popular belief, social sites do not increase human interaction. It may seem like that on the surface, as many of us are connected to hundreds, if not thousands of people at any one time. But you are not interacting with them per se, but rather their digital presence. We act in ways we wouldn't usually do so in person. We say things that we wouldn't in face-to-face interactions. We also get stuck in echo chambers of current belief systems, as algorithms present only what we have previously interacted with. This is the reason why you should never click "like" on random posts. I realized this some time ago. You get re-targeted with all sorts of stuff when you do. The algorithms are busy building a digital map of our behaviors. Don't feed this beast, browse occasionally, but be sparing with your clicks.

Anyway back to the point. Make sure you consolidate your electronic equipment as much as possible. It's not necessary for the average person to own a PC, laptop, digital camera, phone, calculator, compass and an alarm clock anymore. All of this technology and functionality (and much more) has been miniaturized and democratized into one device which fits nicely into your pocket. I now own a laptop (MacBook Air) and my phone (iPhone X), and that's it. Everything is synced and streamlined to perfection concerning power cables and accessories, as well as my data which is stored conveniently in the cloud for just $1 a month. This behavior isn't being a traditionalist or technophobe, but rather the opposite, I.e., a savvy minimalist. It works great when traveling too, but more on this shortly.

I love Apple products for this very reason. They were perhaps the first technology company to embrace minimalism as a philosophy. The original iPod had just one button and a spinner wheel which contained your entire library of CD's. The iPhone did a similar thing for phones. No more clunky keypads, just a touchscreen and again, one button. These products stripped away any excess and left only what was required. Not only that, but they also looked sleek and stylish at the same time. I'm not sure if Steve Job's was a practicing minimalist himself. He certainly had an affinity for Eastern culture, especially the Japanese. It's claimed that his interest in Zen teachings influenced him profoundly when it came to product R&D. What isn't in doubt, is that the company he shaped, certainly played a significant role in transforming the digital tech industry into what we know today.

Media Cleansing

A big reason why I believe that minimalism is gaining such popularity in recent times is the exponential increase in information overload were experience today. This is again a gift and curse when it comes to instant connectivity of our mobile devices. We can be kept up to date with all manner of things throughout the day. Although this can quickly get out of hand if we don't curb our internet use. If we don't satiate our desire for yet more knowledge, or should I say information. As of 2018 statistics, there are 95 million Instagram posts per day. Over 500 million app downloads each day, in addition to over 300 hours of YouTube content uploaded every minute! There is no sign of this slowing down anytime soon either.

The human brain is just not used to computing all of this data at once. For tens of thousands of years, we functioned in largely linear terms. We had to consider the implications of our own circumstance, and perhaps that of our close friends and family group, but that was it. Now we have the whole worlds issues to ponder! Its no wonder we get overwhelmed so quickly now. At some point, it becomes impossible to focus on our daily tasks, and we break down completely. So what's the solution? We need to cut down our exposure to low-quality news and celebrity gossip for a start. We seem to have an unquenchable appetite for this stuff. But is it really doing us any good? I mean, we can't control anything we are reading or hearing about, we are just consuming it. But its worse than that, these topics start to destroy our thinking with worry and doubt.

Stephen Covey illustrates this excellently within his book *"The 7 Habits of Highly Effective People"* wherein he highlights the difference between "Circles of Concern" and "Circles of Control." Circles of concern being the things we spend time professing about but have no control over, I.e., Political scandals, stock market crashes, terrorist attacks and the outcome of Monday night football. Postulating over these things takes time and energy away from working on factors which are in your circle of control, I.e., Your financial situation, health, and current relationship statuses.

I'm not suggesting to become unsympathetic to other peoples problems. But you need to draw the line somewhere. That's what this philosophy is all about. As contrary to what many people believe, the conscious parts of our brains, such as the thought creation and memory centers, do not have infinite capacity. Neuroscientific studies show that we do use heuristics to connect the dots on existing information more efficiently, but at some point, we have to actively forget arbitrary facts and figures to learn and retain new ones. This is why information overload is so critical to avoid.

One of the most important ways we can do this is by sanitizing the devices you have chosen to keep. Along similar lines to cutting down social site time, it's also a good idea to conduct a major spring clean of the applications you are using. This applies to your laptop, iPad, and PC, but most importantly when it comes to your smartphone and for good reason. You will be carrying this one around 24/7, and it can distract you greatly if you let it. The best thing you can do is switch off notifications. I physically have to open apps to view any new activity now. I have to press on my WhatsApp icon to display any new messages for instance. This way I get to respond in my own time and am not continually being distracted by brain farts any one of my contacts has throughout the day. I silence any group chats for the most part too, as they are endless streams of nonsense on steroids!

You should also be cleansing your devices of as many cluttering and time wasting apps as possible. It may seem like a good idea to download Angry Birds for a while, but it can be frightening to calculate just how much time you will spend directing these digital, unhappy, egg-laying animals each day. Studies show that a typical gamer will spend up to 2 hours a day with their face firmly planted to their phone. I've never found the allure of video games, even when I was a kid. I instinctively knew they were a waste of my attention. Why spend all that time involved in some programmers creation? I would always be out and about finding adventure elsewhere, and later developing the skills which would help me be more successful in business. Constantly searching for what can give me the highest ROI on my time. Buts that's just me, maybe I'm an old timer with no sense of fun. I would argue that enjoyment is much better derived from elsewhere anyway, from genuine human interaction. But again, that's just me.

But for the apps you do decide to keep, a good tip is to place them within folders on the home page of your screen. This way you have to press on the folder, then the app icon to open it. It may seem like a small thing, but this additional step adds up over time and significantly reduces your propensity to access it in the first place. I've heard of settings and apps which can now mediate your smartphone use even more stringently than this. They will block access to WhatsApp, Facebook, Instagram, or any site of your choosing for entire periods of the day. This might be useful for those starting out on their quest to break heavy digital addictions. Remember you can always take a planned hiatus from social media. I typically take one full week detox every quarter which helps re-set my head.

Another important area to make inroads is in regards to your email. I have talked already about the importance of clearing any critical correspondence early in the day. In truth, this can be at any time, as long as its predetermined, and you are not checking for new mail every ten minutes. This is a sure fire way to become distracted and get less done. The phrase "crackberry" wasn't invented for no reason. It was devised by the wives of businessmen who become glued to their Blackberry's back in the early 2000's. At the time the PDA/pager device was extremely popular, primarily due to the ergonomically designed keyboard, which made the ease of replying to emails almost instantaneous. If you require the access to your inbox for work, then, by all means, retain emailing apps on your phone. Otherwise, wait until a predetermined time to check them on a laptop instead.

However, you must unsubscribe from any pointless newsletters you may have signed up to in the past. Much like digital games, sifting through endless ramblings of online bloggers, in addition to sales copy from internet marketers, is a monumental waste of time for the most part. I subscribe to only the most essential these days and perform an inbox cleanse every month in order to erase anything which isn't super pertinent to my current situation. Every email will have that little unsubscribe link within the footer, so make use of it and get ruthless in your cull. Otherwise, the disruptions to your day will be endless.

In fact, I hardly ever answer my phone when it rings these days too, especially if I don't recognize the number calling me. Why would I let some sales person interrupt and direct my attention for part of the day? You have to operate on YOUR schedule, not other peoples. I usually just check some voicemail at the same predetermined time that I check my social accounts and emails. I reply to anything important then, and only then. Otherwise its easy to become inundated with messages and requests on what seems like a minute-by-minute basis throughout the day.

Television Time

While online gaming and general internet use are fast catching up to television when looking at the figures, this old media still plays a significant role in most peoples lives. Its found that the typical American household still watches an average of 4.5 hours of TV per day. In addition to this, the number of television sets is also on the rise. As of 2016, this figure exceeded the number of people living in the home. There were now 2.7 TV sets for every 2.5 people. Unlike many staunch minimalists, I'm not against owning a TV entirely. I still have one in my living room, but it's for purely decorational purposes. It hangs off the wall like a 55-inch black mirror for the most part. I do occasionally hook it up to my laptop via an HDMI cable to watch a movie, but that's it.

There is indeed no need for hundreds of cable channels anymore. Not only are they a complete waste of time and money, but they are almost certainly doing your mindset much more harm than good. They call it programming for a reason. I also think there is something fishy going on with television prices. They are so darn cheap now. Amazon will sell you a brand new flat screen for less than your local electronics store, and also ship it to you for free! They, of course, have more efficiency in their logistics chain, but this business model can't continue forever. Somebody somewhere still really wants us watching this stuff, but I'll put my tin foil hat away for now. I'm writing a book on minimalism, not conspiracy theories, so I'll leave it there…

So in general, my advice would be to go straight to the source of information and entertainment you like. Subscribe to your favorite YouTube channels and simply catch up on their content for an hour or so per day at the most. I also have a Netflix subscription as I thought it would simplify and streamline my movie watching, although I'm seriously considering canceling this one too. Binge watching seasons of Narcos can be fun, but I can still find better uses of my time if I'm honest. This will be a personal call for you though. Some people find an hour of escapism at the end of the day helps them switch off from their daily work. They view it as a cathartic experience, and I can't argue with this. Just know what you are getting yourself into. Know how much time you are spending watching programs each day. Never turn on the TV and aimlessly switch through the channels for something to watch. Know the times of your favorite shows and sit down only then. Or record them and watch them at a predetermined time.

You should be seeing a familiar theme to all of this advice by now. To truly create a harmonious life of minimalism not only requires the cutting down of unneeded clutter and activities in your day. But also performing the ones you are left with on YOUR clock and at times which work for YOU.

CHAPTER 6: TRANSPORTATION & TRAVEL

"Minimalism is asking why before you buy."

(Francine Jay)

Transit Tips

I mentioned my beloved BMW 5 series within the introduction to this book. I really enjoyed driving that car, but in reality, it was overkill in terms of space, horsepower, and gas-guzzling ability. It had too much of these things if truth be told. In essence, it cost me far more compared with the payoff it was providing. Many of us fall into this trap while attempting to keep up with the Joneses. I'm not trying to be a killjoy here. Many of you (especially the guys) may have a liking for exotic and fast cars. If this is your thing, then, by all means, get the one you want for a while. But the fact remains, you only really enjoy these things for a while. I want an Aston Martin, but I know I will sell it within a year or two when my young family comes along, as it will just not be practical anymore.

Like everything with this mindset, it's about cutting down to simplify your life. Many believe that it requires selling all of your vehicles and opting for public transport instead. There is some logic behind this. I mean, do you really own your car anyway? Or does it own you? I'm the one who has to service it each year. I'm the one who has to fill it with gas, change the oil and pay for its storage wherever I go. But it just comes down to your personal circumstance. If getting the train, bus, or better yet, cycling to the office works for you, then do it. You will be cutting down your carbon footprint and perhaps getting in shape if you can manage this. But don't make things considerably more painful for yourself if driving the family sedan does the job just fine.

Its really about performing a cost analysis as well as a convenience check. Work out exactly how much your vehicle is costing you in finance and upkeep. The American Automobile Association frequently surveys car owners and found that the average person outlays around $8,5000 per year by owning one. That works out to roughly $700 per month when insurance, taxes, repairs and parking fees are factored in. Again, I'm not saying do away with your vehicle without delay, just clearly understand what it's costing you and where you can make some savings. Can you downsize and pocket yourself some cash? Can you sell your car and make do with using ride-sharing apps such as Uber? For some folks, they can't do away with this mode of transportation entirely for understandable and logistical reasons, and that's just fine. Only you know your current circumstance, just ensure you know your numbers before making any decisions.

Even if you do decide to keep the four wheels. You can always cut down the need to drive it everywhere. I mean, do you really need to drive a mile and a half to the store each day? Or can you take a walk or cycle instead? It's simply a value calculation as always regarding the monetary cost, time efficiency as well as your health. Only once all of these considerations are factored in can you make these decisions wisely. Gone are the days when communities used to help one another out by carpooling to work, or taking turns to taxi kids to and from school. If you're fortunate enough to still enjoy this environment where you live, then make full use of it.

Vacation Considerations

Minimalism is widely considered the practice of tidying up your home and living space. But one of the biggest benefits of clearing out the unneeded clutter from your life is that it allows you to travel more freely, more often, and much lighter when you do. You can save on expensive luggage allowances, take advantage of last minute cheap flight tickets. But most importantly of all, frees you in a psychological sense to enjoy your destination that much more. You can take in the sights and surroundings without the constant need to plan for the logistics of carting around your stuff!

Traveling naturally forces us to return to a minimalist state. You pack your things, grab your passport and head out the door. Yes you might feel that nagging sense that you've forgotten something, but you know it will only be a peripheral item, you have the essentials. You rock up at your hotel room where everything is tidy, and all you need is immaculately laid out for you. These instances are a true minimalist sanctuary for the time being. You are free to put down your stuff and go and explore the city you've found yourself in. However, it can be done incorrectly if you are not careful.

I remember being in Koh Phangan, Thailand some years ago. The island which made full moon parties popular. It's very much a beaten track tourist spot these days, although most young Westerners still travel quite light when they go. But I'll never forget seeing a group of young American girls struggling to haul their ginormous pink suitcases off the long-tail boats, which ferried people to the beach drop off points. I recall thinking to myself "whatever you have in that monstrosity, must really be worth it". In reality, it was almost certainly an abundance of clothes, hairdryers and other pointless accessories unsuited to the humid South-East Asian climate.

So how do you avoid this pitfall yourself? The first thing to do in my opinion begins with getting your packing game right. It all starts from here, and with a little planning as always. Getting yourself one well-organized travel bag is such a wise investment to make. Something medium-sized and durable, which can go in both check-in luggage, or fit into the overhead compartments as a carry on bag. You only need enough space for a selective amount of essential clothes. This number will obviously depend on the length of your trip. It's a good idea to plan for laundry too, in order to cut down the need for excessive garments anyway. I'm a professional at finding local laundry places now, although most hotels will offer this service for a small fee too.

Just pack for what is probable. Get out of the mindset of packing for all possibilities. Getting caught with your pants down in these situations rarely happens. It's not worth planning for it all your life, to satisfy the one time it does happen. There's good fun to be had being able to think on your feet when you need to become resourceful. This concept scares most people, but really, what's the worst that can happen anyway? You have to buy a cheap raincoat that you'll throw away after your trip. Its better than lugging around your heavy and expensive winter jacket everywhere you go "just in case."

Suitcase pockets are always desirable to store your selected items like electronics and toiletries. This is where you can make a significant impact on your minimalist traveling game. Most retail pharmacy stores and supermarkets stock small sized toiletries, I.e., under 100 milliliters, to not only save on space but ensure you pass through security and costumes checks just fine. I've lost countless bottles of shampoo and shaving creams due to the crazy fluids and liquid restrictions of airlines. If you often travel (like me), you can take full advantage of the miniature shampoos and shower gels most hotels will provide. Just take a couple when you leave and fill them up with your own toiletries when you next fly.

With a little planning and foresight, you can make traveling a genuinely enjoyable and stress-free experience again, which its always supposed to have been. You just have to learn to let go and relax. Some of the best times I've spent away are resolving minor mishaps. I never allow room for anything drastic to happen, especially on business trips. But vacations are your time to be free of the worries that even your everyday minimalism lifestyle provides. Travel broadens the mind, so don't deteriorate the experience by worrying about unnecessary stuff. That completely defeats the point of this philosophy entirely!

CHAPTER 7: FOOD - OPTIMIZING YOUR PLATE

By now you should be getting an idea of how to really streamline your life. Ways you can more optimally plan your activities and actions to alleviate psychological baggage in a big way. There is one area that few people consider when it comes to this process though, and that's with regards to their eating habits. Have you ever thought about just how much time you spend feeding yourself on a daily basis? Let alone if you have a small family? Have you ever aggregated the time spent in the grocery store, preparing the food, cooking it, consuming it before cleaning it all up? I can promise you its a lot.

When you add up all of this activity, you quickly realize that a significant portion of your life is dedicated to food. I'm not saying there's a problem with this necessarily. Devising interesting and colorful recipes serves as a favorite past time to some people. Meal times provide a respite from daily work and affords the opportunity to connect with family and friends. These are among the most important occasions for many, I.e., breaking bread with loved ones. So I'm certainly not suggesting to sanitize your eating habits to the point of total efficiency. I just want you to consider the extent of the situation, and as always, get some leverage on yourself where you can.

I'll admit that for me being a single guy when first starting out on my minimalist journey, was a benefit. Everything is easier when only considering yourself, and no more so than when it comes to food. I was working lots and exercising daily. Meal times were regimented time slots designed for utility more than taste. I wanted to get the correct nutrients into my body at the required times, so I could achieve my fitness goals while having enough fuel to make it through the day. The bachelor lifestyle certainly gives you an advantage in this sense. I have a little more thinking to do now that it's my wife and me, but I still do many of the things I did as a single guy, in order to simplify my eating habits.

Streamlined Shopping

This process all starts with your grocery experience. I used to spend hours a week walking up and down the aisles of my nearest Safeway or Whole Foods. I would have to make two trips, once on a Monday, then again on a Friday, as the fridge would be empty come the weekend. I also struggled to carry the amount of bags necessary for an entire weeks shop in one go, hence having to split it up. I now have a much better option. I subscribe to my local supermarket delivery service where I can hop online and order exactly what I want, and they deliver everything to my door before the day is out.

With a little planning, I can select everything I need for the week regarding fresh produce, and use it all before anything goes bad. This way I only have to do my shopping once on a Monday, and I'm good to go. It costs me five bucks in delivery charge, but that's well worth the savings I make in terms of time and effort getting myself to the store twice a week. Just taking into consideration gas money and parking alone, I make that five bucks back already. If you are performing a cost and convenience transport analysis described in the previous chapter, then this is the sort of thing I'm referring to. For me, supermarket delivery services are yet another tick in the "get rid of the car column." Although not quite enough to tip me over the edge to sell it just yet.

Mainly because my wife and I will make a trip to Costco once a month to stockpile the pantry with non-perishables, much like squirrels do before winter time. We will buy canned food, condiments, and the occasional case of wine… or two. Some minimalists will tell you this is overkill, and that you should only be stocking what you require for that week, that day, or even that meal! But this is inefficient, as once again, minimalism isn't solely about less stuff. Its proactively arranging your life to function more smoothly from an activity and time standpoint. Going to a wholesale food outlet once in a while saves me money, as well as an additional four trips to the local supermarket each month.

Selection Secrets

Streamlining your shopping habits is one thing, but optimizing what you are putting in your basket, or selecting in your online cart, is quite another. You want to go simple and organic here as much as possible. Most of the foods we buy are highly processed but undernourished. Yes, it will cost you a little more to purchase these organic ingredients, but you need to decide what's important. Microwave meals and fast food seem like a minimalists dream for making your eating activities more efficient. But what you gain in time, you lose in nutrition. You are likely causing more issues for yourself later on down the line, which is going to cost you a lot more time and money to fix in the future.

I'm no medical doctor or nutritionist, but I know that eating highly processed foods isn't a good idea. I know that if I want to avoid endless trips to the doctors and astronomical medical bills, I need to be eating healthy, whole foods by and large. We should be focusing on the fresh fruit and vegetable aisles much more than you probably have been. Cancer research foundations around the world are continually increasing the amounts of vitamins and anti-oxidants required from these foods, just to stave off the disease. Their current recommendation is anywhere between 12-15 serving a day now! A serving is classed as the size of an average adults fist. But I find anything other than farmers market or certified organic food, do not contain the high levels of nutrients they once did. I can feel the difference immediately when I opt for the higher quality bell peppers, broccoli, and carrots.

This is why we need to switch to clean and unprocessed sources of produce. A wide-ranging and colorful collection of organic fruits and vegetables provides all of the micronutrients we require to remain healthy. They are also highly anti-inflammatory and offer the fiber and roughage to aid digestion in a big way. The typical "Standard American" diet simply does not contain enough of these disease fighting food substances. This is the first thing to get right. After that, its solely about selecting the correct sources of fats, proteins, and carbohydrates to get your macronutrient profile right.

This will differ slightly with regards to the health and fitness goals you are trying to achieve. But a typical macronutrient profile would be around 55%, 30% & 15% relating to carbohydrates, proteins, and fats respectively. There's been a resurgence of Ketogenic style eating habits recently, even full-blown carnivore diets. I'm not here to preach one over the other, I have tried them all in an attempt to optimize my health and nutrition. The one I feel abundantly more happy with is undoubtedly the typical macronutrient make-up I described above. It just requires finding the correct ingredients which is key to feeling great. Obtaining healthy sources of fats from omega-3 rich avocados, nuts, and seeds. Consuming lean sources of poultry and wild caught fish when I do consume animal protein. Eating high grade, low Glycemic Index carbohydrates, from whole grains such as brown rice, quinoa and, simple oats.

I mentioned the Okinawans previously, as they are a special group to study when it comes to longevity. Or at least they used to be. The typical inhabitant of the Japanese island would regularly make it to 100 years old during the early to mid-1900's. This occurrence has primarily been attributed to their diet which consisted of high amounts of clean and fresh produce. Okinawans tended to consume less rice than those on the mainland, with the majority of their calories (circa 70%) coming from purple sweet potatoes instead. The remainder of their calories was coming from legumes and green vegetables, with only around 3% coming from animal products (mainly fish).

However, during the 1950's and 60's, Okinawa saw an influx of Americanized fast food outlets after World War 2 had ended. This started a trend which has seen a gradual decline in the general population's health on the island, which has almost caught up to the dire state of average Western countries today. All markers for mortal health conditions such as cancer and coronary heart disease have gone through the roof since they've adopted our eating habits. You can make your own conclusions from that one.

But its not just what we are choosing to consume which makes the difference. That is only one side of the equation. Just as importantly, we have to identify what we should be getting rid of. What you should be clearing out of the pantry and kitchen cupboards for good. If you are confused about what these undesirable foods are, then you have to look at the contents tab on the back of the packaging. As a rule of thumb, anything with additives including 'ose' or 'syrup' has to go! Dextrose, dextrin, maltodextrin, maltose, high-fructose corn syrup, refiner's syrup, carob syrup and the like.

An excellent minimalist strategy to follow initially is to avoid anything which comes in packaging of any kind. ONLY put organic and whole foods in your basket — essentially anything your grandparents would identify as food. This way you know its simple and clean produce. These foods contain much more nutritional content, as well as being pesticide free, allowing for more efficient mood regulation and reduced inflammation and irritation of the digestive systems. If you are to buy canned food, then ensure there's a maximum of three ingredients contained within them, I.e., Kidney beans, sodium, and water for example.

Prep Like a Pro

If you are anything like me, then you would typically spend a great deal of time contemplating what you are going to eat, and how you'll prepare it. I would open the cupboards and fridge each day and think the same thing "what can I make with this lot then." It was a daily sticking point and an unnecessary step which wasted much time, in addition to ensuring I put together some very bland and uninspiring dishes. I would throw anything together just to get it done. Not anymore though. I have now designed a simple 4-step process to ensure I streamline my meal prep each day, which goes something like this:

Step 1. Identify my meal base, in terms of carbohydrates, I.e., quinoa, whole grain pasta, rice, sweet potatoes, etc.

Step 2. See what vegetables I have available to add, I.e., Broccoli, cabbage, asparagus and the like.

Step 3. Select what protein source I want to use in the dish, I.e., fish, chicken, beef, or legumes for a vegetarian option.

Step 4. Chose which flavoring and seasoning I want to go for, what combination of herbs/spices. Adding in some fresh chili, garlic or perhaps some lemon juice is usually enough although rosemary and thyme are my favorites for Sunday roasts!

Creative Cooking

The trick here is to keep things simple and go back to basics. That doesn't mean tasteless, but it does mean scrutinizing your ingredient list and seeing what combinations work for you. I set myself a rule, I have to prepare each meal with five ingredients or less, and still make it taste great! This book is certainly not intended to be a recipe cookbook, and I'm definitely no Bobby Flay. The aim is simply to give you an idea and outline to follow for yourself.

I cook enough food for around three meals at the very least: one for now, and two that I store in glass containers within the fridge to reheat later in the day or the following one. This way I do the cooking once, but reap the benefit of eating the meal three times. This way I heavily reduce the preparation time beforehand, as well as the washing and cleaning up afterward. It's an essential minimalist time saver and common sense tactic everyone should use. My other pro tip is to embrace shakes. If you don't own a good blender than I highly recommend picking one up.

A substantial shake can pack just as much nutritional content as an entire meal. They taste great and require very little preparation and clean up time. I will have a green smoothie or protein and fruit shake in between meals, especially when I'm on the go. I make enough in the morning to consume as I'm flying out the door, as well as packing one in my bag for later that day. I'll throw in some simple oats, blueberries, half a frozen banana, a scoop of chocolate protein powder, and I'm good to go! You can always place these ingredients (or any of your liking) into a mason jar each evening for some overnight oats too. It works just the same.

The key to all of this is not over thinking things, but rather to embrace simplicity instead. Food prep and consumption can become overwhelming if you let them. But with a little planning and adjustment to your routines, you can streamline your eating habits to not only save you a great deal of time and effort but also get your health and nutrition in order too. You will find that you will no longer crave sugary and processed foods if you can successfully make this switch. I now have so much more stamina throughout the day, allowing me to enjoy the activities that much more, which is the ultimate minimalist goal.

CHAPTER 8: EXERCISE - GETTING MORE BANG FOR YOUR BUCK

I have always been an active and sporty person. I played football three times a week while growing up, which continued through college. I now go to the gym four times a week as well as swim on a consistent basis. But it certainly gets a little more difficult as I age. It's tougher to drag myself to the gym on those cold January nights after a long days work. In this sense, it's now more important than ever that I optimize my training sessions to continue reaping the rewards from them. This is where my minimalist mindset has helped immensely. I will always make time for physical exercise, and for good reason.

Much like fixing your eating habits and diet, doing a proper amount of physical activity can have huge payoffs in other areas of your life. You feel fitter and stronger which makes all other daily tasks that much easier to complete. It also makes you feel great from a psychological and mental health perspective. Regular workouts produce mood improving compounds such as dopamine and serotonin, while simultaneously reducing the stress hormone cortisol. There really isn't a reason not to undertake at least a moderate amount of physical activity to remain in good health. But similar to my advice regarding diet, I'm not here to preach, but simply give you my 2 cents and what has worked for me.

Being a minimalist doesn't mean that I follow the same old boring workouts though. As with the food I eat, I like to keep it varied but straightforward from day-to-day to ensure things remain exciting and fresh. But this doesn't mean you have to over complicate the matter either. The key to exercise is consistency and continually aiming for progress. We are not striving for Olympic lifting records here, or trying to run sub-4-minute miles. Just pushing yourself enough to achieve some progressive overload, and ensure the body is improving and adapting to the stimulus you are subjecting it to when working.

So how can the everyday person do this? Studies show that it takes only around 20-30 minutes of work to elicit the desired response we are looking to achieve. In fact, they indicate that as little as 12 minutes will do the job if the activity is intense enough. But to err on the safe side, I usually recommend people do no less than 20 minutes of exercise at any one time, to make sure they aren't undercutting themselves too much. If you are going to get a workout session in, you might as well do it properly. As minimalist's, we want to optimize our time as much as possible, but that doesn't mean being lazy.

So whether you are performing a cardiovascular routine, strength building or muscle conditioning. You have to work hard enough and tax the body effectively during this time, in order to provide an adequate stimulus and initiate a recovery response, which ultimately provides the adaptations we want. You just need to focus on the basics and get your body moving to begin with here. The good news is that this can be done at home with a small set of dumbbells and body weight movements (push-ups, pull-ups, sit-ups, etc). Cardio work can be performed with a run around the block. If your fitness goals are a little loftier than you will have to get yourself to the gym for some proper equipment and a bit more time commitment. But more on this later.

In general, the minimalist workouts require targeting large muscle groups with compound movements to get the most bang for your exercising buck. Forget bodybuilder style isolation movements such as bicep curls and leg extensions. Functional compound lifts will incorporate all muscle groups just fine while utilizing your time and energy much more efficiently too. Things like chest and shoulder press, seated row, and dumbbell/body weight squats, will improve your strength in these everyday movements. You need to be able to carry the groceries and move the furniture when clearing out your minimalist house after all! You can also travel with these simple workout routines, especially if only utilizing body weight for instance.

If you have no idea where to start with your exercising activities, then the following beginner workout (complete with its variations), should give you an idea of how to get going:

20-Minute Minimalist Home Workout

The Warm-Up (2.5 minutes)

This portion is designed to get your heart rate up safely. Also to get your body loose, and some blood flowing to the muscles, priming them for some rigorous activity ahead. From the literature and articles that I've read, it's best to save any serious stretching to your cool down session. Studies show that anything more than a 5-6 second stretch will encourage pooling of blood in the muscles, and actually inhibit performance. So stick to a quick stretch if you have to here. Its much more important to do a short jog, cycle or row if you have the equipment. If not, a set of star jumps, jumping jacks or burpees will do just fine! Just get yourself to the point of shortness of breath, where it would be difficult to have a conversation with someone standing next to you. This should be the sweet spot regarding readiness to jump into your full session, I.e., at roughly 70% of your maximum working heart rate.

The Workout (15 minutes)

Now its time to really ramp things up. You have two choices here, either a resistance style workout with dumbbells and body weight or cardiovascular style circuits. Each will be performed in an interval training sense, I.e., short bursts on intense activity followed by a short rest period. You can adjust this to suit your own fitness levels, to begin with. Start with 30-second working sets, followed by 1 minute rest periods. Then slowly switch this around as the weeks go by, giving yourself more working time, and less rest.

An example might be as follows:

Workout 1: (Cardio based)

30-second hill sprints, followed by

A 1-minute walk back down to the starting line

(Repeat this sequence for the entire 15 minutes)

Workout 2: (Resistance based)

30-seconds of squats into shoulder press with 5kg dumbbells (I.e., Clean & Press)

Followed by a 1-minute rest

30-seconds of press ups

Followed by a 1-minute rest

30-seconds of twisted leg lunges

Followed by a 1-minute rest

(Repeat this sequence for the entire 15-minutes)

Workout 3: (Combination of Cardio & Resistance)

2-minutes bicycle, followed by

A 1-minute rest

30-seconds of chin ups (assisted if needed)

Followed by a 1-minute rest

2-minutes bicycle, followed by

A 1-minute rest

30-seconds of dumbbell goblin squats

Followed by a 1-minute rest

(Repeat this sequence for the entire 15 minutes)

These are considered HIIT style workouts which stands for (High, Intensity, Interval, Training). As I mentioned, these routines recruit the largest muscle groups and tax the bodies cardiovascular systems to maximize metabolic response. The key is performing cyclical bursts of intense activity, followed by a rest and recovery period. This type of workout is perfect for a minimalist trying to get the most out of their sessions. They are best performed as full body routines. However, you can split them up into variations of your liking, perhaps focusing on cardiovascular work one day, and resistance sets the next or by combining the two.

The Cool Down (2.5 minutes)

Just like warming up before your session, it's also important to cool the body down after intense interval workouts. Doing so will help return the heart rate to near resting levels, as well as drain the muscles of metabolic waste products such as lactic acid. You merely need to perform a few minutes of sustained lower intensity steady exercise, I.e., the opposite of the high impact stuff within your main session. A light jog moving into a brisk walk works great for me.

I also finish my sessions with a 1-minute flow yoga routine too. It helps stretch the muscles and relaxes the mind all in one go. But more on these relaxation techniques next. My advice would be to perform these workouts every other day, to begin with, and see how you respond and recover to them. If you feel good, then do a variation of the HIIT style routines every day. Remember that it will only take 20 minutes total, and everyone can fit that into their schedule regardless of how busy you are. It just comes down to priorities.

Advanced Workouts

For the advanced athletes and gym rats among you, you may soon outgrow the beginner minimalist home workouts. If this is the case, you simply have to up the intensity of these workouts by heading to the gym where there is some more serious equipment. You can lift more weight more safely in these environments. You can also double the length of workout to 40 minutes too, but no more. Studies show that this is about the maximum a human can work before benefits radically start to drop off. The "pump" will dissipate indicating that blood flow is leaving the musculature.

Depending on the amount of carbohydrates you've consumed earlier that day, energy levels tail off to the point they need to be replenished with intra-workout carbs. I typically find that my motivation starts to wain at this point too, so its time to jump in the shower and get on with my day. Not overtaxing myself also ensures that my central nervous system has time to recover fully, enabling me to perform at maximum effort within the next 24-48 hours.

With that said, I would suggest doing one of these workouts every other day, to ensure you recover fully. This advice is especially relevant for those in their late 30's and above (like me). If you're in your 20's then you can get away with blasting 2-3 days in a row more than likely. I'm actually not that disappointed about my slight drop off in performance as I age. It forces me to plan my sessions more optimally in line with my minimalist lifestyle. Gone are the days of spending 2 hours in the gym five days a week. Now I'm in and out in 45 minutes before resuming my daily schedule. I feel that I get just as much achieved in these streamlined sessions and certainly feel better than ever.

But whatever you decide to do, it's important just to get yourself moving to begin with here. Of course, your own lifestyle, work, and family commitments will be factored into this. The guidelines here are just that, an overview to get you started. Many minimalists find that at some point it's wise to hire a personal trainer too, as they will push you harder than working out on your own. It's a great way to maximize your time in the gym even further, ensuring your sessions are that much more efficient and worthwhile. What you'll pay in money, you'll gain back in results I assure you.

CHAPTER 9: MINIMALISM MIND TECHNIQUES

"The best things in life aren't things."

(Anonymous)

I often get asked for the one thing that would help people succeed when attempting to create a life of minimalism for themselves. But the answer is not what you might think it would be. Most folks expect that I'll tell them to become good at throwing stuff away, arranging their living space or learning to be happy with less. These are all vital elements. Reducing the burden of excessive possessions while budgeting correctly for what you do have, is a fantastic way to create more freedom in life. But there is a stage which comes before all of this tangible organizational and logistical practices. You have to get in the correct state of mind before you can complete any of these tasks. It takes an adjustment in thinking to make the most significant strides towards a minimalist lifestyle.

In my experience, there aren't any better methods to achieve this than by applying meditation and mindfulness practices. I've tried everything while coming to this conclusion. What I have found is that clearing the mind of endless postulation is paramount for well-being. These techniques allow us to get back to our true selves, its the ultimate stripping away of the unneeded. Its pure existence, we simply become one with our environment. Nature doesn't worry about the past or fret about the future, that's exclusively a human ailment. It just exists, where nothing needs to be done, but everything gets done.

But this isn't meant to be some spiritual or metaphysical manuscript. But rather a practical playbook to make minimalism a reality in your life, and there honestly isn't a more vital space to clear, than that which is in your mind. Therefore, this chapter contains some of the tried and tested psychological strategies on how to do this successfully. It doesn't matter if you do not have any experience with meditation or mindfulness training. You have to start somewhere, and literally, any amount of practice will help to begin with.

The following exercises have aided me greatly in developing more clarity and peace of mind. They have brought a calmness to my life and helped me develop the landscape for true minimalist thinking to flourish. There's a misconception that meditation means you will be sitting around all day contemplating the universe and nothing more. Yes, at some stage in your life you may genuinely become enlightened and no longer wish to partake in earthly activities. I got a glimpse of this during a 10-day Vipassana silence retreat while on the same Thailand trip, I mentioned previously. The initial three days of these experiences are quite tricky to manage, even for regular meditators. Being alone with your thoughts for 10 hours a day without communicating with anyone is such a stark contrast to the average working Westerners day. It can be quite harrowing in fact. You will continuously be contemplating your current issues, relationship statuses, the state of your financial situation, as well as upcoming projects you want to get working on.

But after the second or third day, things start to change. The mind gets used to the silence and surrenders to the situation. You've thought everything through 1000 times by now, and are more easily able to let go. I felt like I was hyper-sensitive to my surroundings and my body. I could intimately feel every sensation in my fingertips down to my toes and focus on them for hours at a time. I also felt in tune and one with some form of universal consciousness which connects us all. However, it doesn't take long for you to come back down to earth when you leave these places. Which is totally fine, as it's not possible to function like that in the real world yet, and I'm not suggesting you try. What I am prescribing here are the practical and everyday methods to help you achieve a minimalist mindset for your daily life. So let's begin with the first strategy.

Meditation Training

First of all its important to point out that these three concepts are far from mutually exclusive. There's much overlap between them, but enough difference to separate them into three slightly different and distinct sections. The first of these is meditation in the traditional sense. Unless you've been living under a rock all these years, you will have at least come across the idea of meditating. You will likely have friends or family who've tried it and can profess to the plethora of benefits it can provide.

Scientists have now been confirming what Eastern practitioners have been claiming all along, that meditation makes physical changes to the brain. When participants are studied under MRI scans, there is a significant increase in gray matter after just 6-8 weeks of guided meditation practice. Not only this, but it also helps rewire the brain in a process known as neuroplasticity. Meditation strengthens the billions of connections and synapses within the system improving memory and creativity all at the same time. Other upsides include preserving brain function as we age, contributing to a reduction of debilitating conditions such as Alzheimer's disease. Combine meditation practice with a healthy diet and you can notice a huge difference. Clean food helps to clear and expand capillaries increasing blood flow to the brain complimenting this whole process.

So how can you gain these amazing benefits for yourself? How do you practice these meditation methods at home? There are many forms available to us. These include Transcendental, Guerrilla & Vipassana I mentioned above. But my favorite is always the simplest, as it can be implemented easily by the everyday person, and in almost any situation. If you can find a quiet spot and sit in the lotus position then even better. Just ensure you have a straight back and can comfortably hold your hands in your lap wherever you may be.

Then it requires initially paying attention to everything that's happening around you, all of the sights, sounds, and distractions. Now close your eyes and aim to focus on just one element of your current circumstance, such as your breath, in order to enter a peaceful, meditative state. But most importantly of all, ensuring that you keep all attention on the present moment. Then if your focus does indeed drift for a second, bring it back to that one element, I.e., the breath, which re-centers you immediately. There is no set time limit to this exercise and the more the better to begin with. I find that setting a timer to anywhere between 10-20 minutes is a good starting point, and ensure you are not falling asleep during this time. I now perform two 20 minute sessions within my day, the first immediately after waking up and the second during lunchtime to realign myself. This may sound like a big time commitment, but its really not. Minimalism is about making space for what is essential and meditation certainly falls into this category. In truth, it actually creates more time in my experience, as it allows me to function that much better in the activities I do choose to partake in. Remember that it's just as important to manage our energy, not simply your time.

So with that said, just give this simple method a go if you have never tried anything like this up to now. Meditation is not an easy thing to master, but once you reach at least a working level of proficiency, it's a powerful tool, especially for a practicing minimalist. If you find it too tricky, you can always seek the help of an expert to guide you. There are many excellent books on the topic which delve into its practices and benefits in much more detail than I can here. So my advice is to do your research and start down the road on your meditation journey.

There are many experienced practitioners who you can learn from in this respect. My personal favorites over the years include Thich Nhat Hanh, a Vietnamese monk whose teachings have enlightened many who have read his work. But also Eckhart Tolle, the author of *"The Power of Now"* for a more contemporary view on things. Some see him as a new age, esoteric self-help guru. Others believe him to be an important spiritual sage, capable of transforming the negative thinking patterns which plague many of our societies today. As always, I would just suggest to be open-minded and try these things. You don't know what you are missing out on otherwise.

Mindfulness Strategies

In essence, mindfulness is defined as the awareness of the present moment. Its roots stem from Buddhism, but similar concepts can be found in just about every contemplative literature and teachings. Mindfulness sounds like an oxymoronic statement. It suggests that the mind is "full" of thoughts when the exact opposite is the case. It simply means to quiet the mind and become fully aware of the feelings which do arise, much like the meditation practice I previously described. The key is to acknowledge all thoughts initially and without judgment.

That's not to say this is an easy task though. In fact, it's virtually impossible for the average person to do on first attempt. We are used to living our lives at 100 miles per hour speeds, and without a seconds pause. Its estimated that we think around 50,000-70,000 thoughts per day! From the studies I've seen, over 90 percent of these are made up of ideas we had the previous day. And around 80% are negative in nature. This concept is known as the negativity bias to psychologists.

The theory states that humans are very much hardwired to focus in on adverse outcomes. The amygdala (a primal component of the brains limbic system) zeros in on the potential dangers we face, as it was so important to do so from an evolutionary standpoint. Our survival depended on directing attention to these situations. If you attributed rustling in the bushes to the movements of a saber-toothed tiger, then you had time to react. If you dismissed it as the wind and it wasn't, then you were removed from the gene pool. But we no longer live in times where a physical threat is hiding around every corner. This is another software upgrade the wetware in our head hasn't yet made, which is why it's so imperative to clear the mind as much and as often as you can.

I certainly struggled with achieving true states of mindfulness, or "No Mind" as its often referred to, especially when starting on the road to authentic minimalism. I would notice that my mind was constantly clogged with these thoughts and themes on repeat. I would struggle when attempting to silence it. I was always worrying about the future. I wondered if I would have enough money to pay the bills, or if I would ever find the perfect partner for me. I would also play out past scenarios in my head and stress about how and where I went wrong. There is some merit in fixing past trauma, but from my experience, it's simply best to forget about it and move on. If any of this sound familiar, then don't worry, you are certainly not alone.

I would task myself to entirely clear my mind of thoughts for just ten seconds. This may sound like an easy feat, but for me, it wasn't! Give it a go for yourself now. Don't move on with your day until you can sit in your current seat, and hold no thought whatsoever for the next 10-15 seconds. Pull over to the side of the road if you are driving while listening to the audio version of this book. If you are anything like me, it will take you a good 15 minutes before you can achieve this on first attempt. But once you can, it becomes far easier the next time around. I can now bring in this state of mindfulness almost on demand, and for minutes at a time when I do. But how can you practice this for yourself?

You can achieve mindfulness by following the meditation techniques I've described already. But you will come up with your own methods in time. I like to think of a little man inside my head who is holding out his arms much like a traffic warden would. I envisage him physically holding back the thoughts from entering my mind. Only when I let him put his arms to his sides, do the feelings start to come in. This way you train them to be patient. It shows them that they do not have complete rule over you. YOU decide when you want to acknowledge and deal with your thoughts. Think about it for a second; you wouldn't let anyone and everyone charge into your home all day long, would you? So why are you allowing this to occur within your mind?

Much of this has to do with separating your true self from the thinker within you. They are not the same thing. The conscious being who experiences life in its raw sense is different from the person who is interpreting everything. The conscious mind is excellent when it comes to planning and strategizing, but that's it. Don't let it run amuck by endlessly scrutinizing past events or future situations. The key is to let it do its thing, before switching off for the day. Much like only answering my emails at predetermined times, I only allow myself to postulate problems within a specified time period too. Then its back to meditation and mindful practices to bring me into the present moment once more.

Breathing Techniques

The third and final strategy you can employ when attempting to hone your minimalism mind training isn't really a psychological practice. But rather a physical exercise which compliments the two previous mind clearing techniques so well which is why I have chosen to include it here. It can also be performed as a standalone exercise, so it does require some individual consideration. It improves the quality of your mentality greatly when done correctly. So how can we best utilize proper mindful breathing for ourselves?

Firstly, it's important to note that breathing is very much an unconscious act for the most part. Various internal mechanisms control the rate and depth of our breath with regards to what we are doing. Increased physical activity will stimulate these triggers in order for us to obtain greater levels of oxygen while expelling increasing amounts of carbon dioxide. These same systems will automatically down-regulate breathing when we are resting or sleeping for the opposite reasons. This activity allows us to function and survive without interruption to our normal daily activities. But this is not what we are talking about here.

We are considering a way to consciously affect our breathing to produce a heightened experience which is most conducive to mindful living. You can't do this all day, but much like segmented meditation practice, it can be implemented at various preset times. You simply have to prepare a little, and it helps to sit up straight in an open posture to aid air flow in and out of your lungs more efficiently. Also, ensure you are breathing in through your nose when inhaling to help cleanse the air of impurities. When exhaling, you can either go back through the nose or the mouth when performing regular deep breathing.

Just try to breathe as deeply as possible contracting the diaphragm and expanding your stomach during the inhalation phase. Then gently let it collapse back down during exhalation. This should feel more intense and deliberate compared with normal shallow breathing. It will trigger an immediate calmness within you, as well as center you as I've already mentioned. Your cells become flooded with excess oxygen in addition to removing bodily toxins. I also find it reduces my blood pressure and improves digestion as an added benefit. Once you are familiar with more intentional breathing, I suggest trying the 4-7-8 method I learned from yoga.

You simply begin by exhaling any air from your lungs. Then start by breathing in through your nose for a count of 4 seconds, followed by 7 seconds of holding the breath and finally exhaling through the mouth for 8 seconds. Repeat this cycle four times to begin with (this can go up to 8 cycles maximum when accustomed to it). When done correctly it produces a slightly altered state of consciousness. Some might feel a little lightheaded at first, but this will pass after some getting used to the process. It should definitively induce a sense of internal relaxation. Hence why its great to try when you get cut off in traffic or wake during the night and find it difficult to go back to sleep.

All of the advice contained within this chapter is aimed at helping you reduce unwanted anxiety and stress within your life. The practices described are proven, and their benefits are no longer in doubt. The only question is, will you also make use of them too? You should be answering this with a quick and resounding YES. Don't get discouraged if you don't feel these positive effects immediately. Stick with it, and you'll start to have those "aha" moments when you least expect it.

CHAPTER 10: CLEARING NEGATIVE THOUGHT PATTERNS

So clearing your head of needless "Monkey Mind" chatter a couple of times a day, as well as intentionally controlling your breathing, is a great starting point for gaining back clarity and control over your thoughts. But it usually doesn't take long before this negative cloud returns to muddy the waters of our thinking. We begin to let fears and worries creep back in, and the mental unrest starts all over again. You can use the techniques in the previous chapter to recenter yourself. Or you can try some additional strategies to help solve the problem. I like to attack this issue from all angles. This includes eliminating emotional reactions and correcting negative thought patterns. Both debilitating factors if they aren't controlled properly.

Reducing Emotional Reactions

As we've already discussed, humans are inherently emotional creatures. The feelings we experience help us navigate the world in just about every sense. But you have to learn to control them otherwise your life can be a never-ending roller coaster ride of highs followed by the lows. I'm not suggesting to reduce emotions to the point of becoming robotic. Just to take stock of what you are currently feeling on a moment-to-moment basis and to correct the wild swings which can cause the most distress. Bottling up or sweeping things under the rug never works in the long term. But that doesn't mean that you have to react to them right away either.

My typical advice to overly sensitive people is not to react, but to respond. What do I mean by this? Everyone has heard the opinion that you should take a moment and count to ten if something has affected you intensely. This is easier said than done in heated situations. But this small pause should ensure that any response is more measured. The Old Zen Master has a great tip for you in this regard which we'll get onto within the chapter on learning to let go. But for now, let's just say its better to give yourself a small window before reacting to highly charged events. If its something I want to revisit later I will do. But I'll do so within the comfort of my own home. That is where I allow myself to experience any anger or grief for instance. It's far better to delay these reactions and leave the heavy emotion until later in the day when you can reflect on it without looking like an emotional wreck in front of people. But most folks walk around in somewhat of a waking sleep. They are entirely at the mercy of any feeling, thought or emotion which pops into their head. So how do we go about fixing this?

1. Acknowledge your feelings

The first thing to do is to become a master at acknowledging and perceiving the emotions that you are feeling. Whenever I feel something arise within me, I always take a second to recognize it. I pause to understand and label it in my mind. This doesn't mean that I'm reacting to it just yet, but I want to know why it has surfaced and if the emotion is beneficial or not. If it's a feeling of stress, worry or frustration, I do not deny or suppress it completely, but rather acknowledge its presence and dismiss it as not being helpful and move on.

If you make a habit of dwelling on these emotions, you will quickly fall into a negative thinking spiral which can have you framing the entire situation in a pessimistic light in no time. This is the reverse of how a happy and sane individual should be functioning. If on the other hand its an emotion of excitement, joy or love, I also pause for a second, and appreciate what I'm experiencing. I like to cultivate and utilize these moments as the feelings are much more conducive to not only my minimalist mindset but a healthy psychological state in general.

But whatever you are feeling throughout the day, it's critical to take responsibility for these emotions, good and bad. Understand that they're coming from inside of YOU and that you and only you can deal with them. This is usually the most challenging step for people but its also the most rewarding. Yes, it may be some external influence which has sparked the response in the first place but remember that it's your responsibility to deal with them.

2. Learning how to forgive

Along similar lines as letting go of negative emotions, people tend to hold onto evil acts performed against them. This can be damaging when its an outside influence like a close friend or family member. Although it can be just as harmful when its an act of our own doing which needs to be forgiven. Retaining this ill feeling serves absolutely no purpose to you now or at any point in the future. "Holding onto anger is like drinking poison and expecting the other person to die" as the Buddha wisely points out.

If you want to reduce the amount of cognitive work you have to perform in a day, you really need to learn the art of forgiveness. If you have been taking on-board the advice regarding relationships ROI's, then you should already be cutting down the physical time you spend with negative people. But if you are still carrying them around in your head, then what's the use? You wouldn't let these people live rent-free in your house, so why are you allowing them to roam freely in your mind? Again, the most natural thing you can do is learn to resent people less for any perceived past wrongdoings and move on. This isn't for their benefit but rather for the sake of your sanity.

3. Stop self-deprecating behavior

In some sense being a little self-deprecating can be a positive trait. It indicates that we do not take ourselves too seriously which is one of the keys to not becoming anxious and stressed to begin with. But letting negative self-talk get out of hand is a terrible habit indeed. It happens far too often as unfortunately many of us still have much work to do when it comes to improving our own self-worth. We often talk ourselves out of things before we've had a chance to give them a go. "This minimalist living seems great for some, but I need my possessions to be happy" you might hear others claim. People instinctively feel unease at getting rid of their belongings as it leaves them naked to the world. They often fill this void with sex, alcohol, drugs and excess material possessions to try and make-up for these perceived inadequacies.

But the payoff from these vices are always short-lived and never the long-term solution. They paper over momentary cracks in our mentality. But as always, we need to get to the root of what really makes us happy and fulfilled in this world which comes from clarity of thought and genuine human connection.

4. Don't judge others (or yourself) too harshly

You must also try to be as non-judgemental as much as possible. This includes not partaking in needless gossip. No longer talking about others in a negative light freed me in a psychological sense when I managed to stop this behavior some years ago. I never thought of myself as an overly judgmental person, but I still caught myself doing it from time-to-time. Preventing yourself from judging people will save you so much mental energy and almost certain daily miss reading of situations.

Nowadays I merely let others go about their lives without even the slightest judging thought about their behavior. That is not to say that I tolerate bad behavior, or don't try to evaluate someone's personality. I just do not judge them with regards to how they got to where they are. I never walked in their shoes or went through the struggles they did, so I give others the benefit of the doubt instead. Again, not for their convenience but for the good of my own mental state.

That is what its really all about. If you can put these mindset principles into practice, you will eventually achieve a much more stable emotional state. You will find balance in your thinking and massively reduce stress levels throughout the day. You will clear your mind of this cognitive baggage that you have been carrying around and create a space which is much more fertile for a minimalist lifestyle to function.

Correcting Negative Thinking Cycles

Much like our modern day digital technology, human cognition is also a double-edged sword. Being able to think things through thoroughly is simultaneously a person's best friend and worst enemy. As we've already seen, humans tend to profess over everything in life. In my opinion "over-thinking" is the worst of all our shortcomings. The brain is extremely complex and is required to perform an unfathomable number of calculations every second: everything from mundane motor skills, to critical and complex decision making.

However, we still do not fully understand the extent of its inner workings. One thing we do know is that the brain is solely responsible for enabling people to develop thinking patterns and habits which ultimately dictate our daily behaviors. It does this in an attempt to optimize day-to-day movements and thought processes. This may sound like a perfect situation for an aspiring minimalist who is attempting to reduce their cognitive workload. But these shortcuts aren't always beneficial.

In order to form these "loops" or "patterns," the brain undertakes several processes which help it both develop a certain habit and make it a part of our routines. But habits are impartial; they will either help a person attain favorable results or ensure they continue getting the negative outcomes they've always gotten. As Dr. Richard Bandler points out "Brains aren't designed to get results; they just go in directions." It's up to us to steer the ship to a favorable destination. That's the good news, to know that we are ultimately in control.

Learning Our ABC's

In this regard, it's simply a matter of learning our ABC's, I.e., determining the sequence of the Antecedent, Behavior, and Consequence. This concept was initially based on B.F Skinner's model of cognition, which em-compasses these three main steps involved in developing a habit. They are interesting elements to know if you want to understand why we do what we do. But more importantly how we can change our behavior for the better. Antecedents are stimuli which precede our actions. They are situations and circumstances which causes a person to behave in a particular manner. They determine how we will react.

Behavior is then the response provided to this stimulus. It's meant to serve two main purposes, namely to get something that a person desires, or to avoid getting something they do not. It's also important to note that almost all behavior is learned from society and significant others which is why I always state that consumerist tendencies can be broken if we know how to handle them properly.

Finally, the consequence is a result of our normal behaviors. This phase can be viewed as the environment's reaction to our daily activity. For example, if a person reacts to a situation in an aggressive manner, then the consequence is typically negative too. If you always react angrily to your spouse not agreeing with you, you can always expect an argument to ensue. Much like evaluating your emotional responses, it's simply about understanding the cues and identifying your triggers which stimulate behavior. Then you can predictably determine the results you will be getting.

This is how we typically form habits in our thinking which can be very powerful cycles, especially if built and reinforced over a long period of time. It isn't necessarily a bad thing if this thought loop is genuinely a beneficial one. But if it's not, then it can be quite destructive. We can see this very clearly in individuals with high obsessive-compulsive tendencies

(OCD). In any case, these cycles can be easily broken with the right strategy. So how do we do this?

Thought Pattern Interrupts

The idea is to disrupt a negative thought pattern as early on in the cycle or sequence as possible, ideally as soon as its triggered. Pattern interrupts aren't difficult to implement, and it's merely about stopping your train of thought and thinking about something different. It's a case of "butting in" on the thought process occurring within your head. You are simply trying to change the direction of the mind and reprogram it as you do. You are not removing the old pattern completely, but instead redirecting around it.

The following are some suggestions to ensure this process works efficiently. Try rubbing your tummy or swapping your watch from one wrist to the other when you start to notice yourself thinking in this negative manner. These subtle disruptions can work well for some people especially for minor mishaps in their thinking. Some more extensive and ingrained negative tendencies can require a bigger interrupter such as loud hand clap or shout. This can look weird in public I will admit!

If none of these techniques work, I'll usually begin a meditation session or even my 20-minute minimalist workout. Both of these practices always puts me back into a positive state of mind. You simply need to find what works for you. Just don't hold back when you do try these methods and repeat the interrupts until they become habitual. Studies show that it takes at least 21 days for a new behavior to take hold. So don't become discouraged if you can't crack this one right away. Stick with it, and at some point, you'll be able to rectify your thinking on demand just like any new skill.

CHAPTER 11: BELIEF SYSTEM RESET

Lastly, I think it's important to discuss one more topic when it comes to minimalism mind techniques, which has to do with the current belief systems we all hold. I studied a good amount of psychology within my undergraduate degree, and have read a lot of popular psychology since then. One of these areas included Neuro-Linguistic Programming or NLP for short. I don't want to make this a white paper on the subject, but needless to say that NLP is a powerful concept when practically implemented in a person's life. One of the founding notions is that "The map isn't the territory." The reality is that a plot of land is a plot of land, but depending on how you view it, it can look completely different. A road map, topographic map, and thematic map will give you a totally different picture of the same "reality." Another way of saying this is that "Perception is Projection."

Everyone will have a different upbringing and set of experiences and will literally be regurgitating that conditioning onto any situation. You can get quite deep into Schrödinger's cat thought experiments or the double slit observations within quantum mechanics. These experiments suggest that we may actually create our entire physical existence through our thoughts and observations. But that's a far more in-depth discussion for another time.

But suffice to say that your belief systems are very important as they determine how you view the world and subsequently how you will act within it. As we have already discussed within the visualization and goal setting segment, most people are driven by unconscious or subconscious belief systems by and large. Much of this conditioning was picked up during childhood, often very limiting beliefs about ourselves which can be very difficult to spot and remove later on in life. They usually play out in continuous cycles of self-sabotaging behavior (without the person realizing it). We certainly have a propensity to consume material things and gather clutter of all kinds within our lives.

The Realization I had About Beliefs

So the major epiphany I had regarding beliefs, is that although they are typically very strong, they usually have no real bearing on what is actually true about the world. But this doesn't matter to most people, as they function just fine sticking to their own ideas. This is because we form our beliefs not because they are necessarily correct, but as they are a guidance system to navigate through the many data points of life. You start to realize this as you age and get proved wrong about things that you were utterly certain on. This realization only has to happen a handful of times for you to honestly assess the validity of your deep held positions.

"I'm a wise man as I know that I know nothing."

(Aristotle)

Much like your emotions and thought patterns, what matters more is if your current beliefs are of benefit to you. They can both be holding you back or propelling you forward. The key is to be continually assessing them, and again, know if they are serving you or not. They are merely an egoic human trait we need to function in the physical world. In this sense, beliefs aren't necessarily something to be proud of, which is especially true if we become dogmatic about them. Doing so ensures we become lazy and myopic in our thinking. To say that your mind cannot be changed regardless of the evidence. As a minimalist, I always want to cut down the cognitive work I need to do on a day-to-day basis, but I want to know if I'm going wrong and how to improve things whenever possible. This attitude is what led me to this philosophy in the first place.

Many people struggle with this advice as they have become so ingrained in their current thought patterns, that they defend them to the death. This type of thinking only causes much mental anguish though. It certainly isn't conducive to providing a favorable environment for your meditation and mindfulness practices to do their best work. This is different from not having any conviction. I don't suggest to change your mind with the wind. I'm proposing to be open to all possibilities before identifying what your own beliefs are. Most people are prisoners to their thoughts and are desperate to be proved "right" regarding them. I often see people becoming so entrenched in their ideas and positions these days. But what they gain in resoluteness, they lose in intellectual honesty.

This is where minimalism can help. It allows a person to clear the mind, evaluate things much more objectively, and surrender to situations more easily. An ability which comes more naturally with age I will admit. "I used to think I knew all of the answers, and now I realize I didn't even know the questions" is a common statement uttered by those in there 40's, when looking back at their 20's. This is again why we need to analyze beliefs so carefully. They're great if they're contributing to your overall happiness and success in life, but can be horrible if they aren't. So the good news is that you can change them if you wish. You are allowed to do that you know. It's a liberating feeling when you understand that beliefs are just a thinking tool and nothing more. So choose them wisely!

"Your beliefs become your thoughts,

Your thoughts become your words,

Your words become your actions,

Your actions become your habits,

Your habits become your values,

Your values become your destiny."

(Mahatma Gandhi)

I simply apply the same minimalist lens over the beliefs I have. I want to hold only a few in my mind, but they should be clear and robust values which help guide my life. One belief I now adamantly adhere to is that I do not need to compare myself to everyone else. Doing so only produces anxiety and unease within us. You will always come up short in some department. I'm not suggesting to not better yourself or strive to higher ideals. But don't continuously nitpick every part of your situation. This very much ties in with my opening remarks to this book regarding the constant need for social proof from others. Or buying newer and more expensive possessions to signal our status.

We all want to be accepted and liked. But this is just a projection of low self-esteem in my opinion. I'm not unkind or impolite to anyone, but I'm not out to impress either. It's much easier for me if I have fewer friends and acquaintances now. I like to retain a close-knit circle who I spend time within their company. I don't want to be continually worrying about how the person I just met on the street perceives me. Its said that "it's not the person with the most possessions who wins the game of life, but he who has the most people at his funeral." This sounds like a sensible minimalist statement. But its only half correct in my eyes. Why is it great to have lots of people at your wake? It signifies that you spent way too much time trying to please anyone and everyone you came across. Just think of what else you could have been doing with your time!

But I'm an introvert by nature, so this notion comes more natural to me. Don't get me wrong; I like other peoples company. It just has to be the right people and in the right amounts. I certainly don't need constant attention to be happy. Being alone isn't the same as being lonely. I know people who find it impossible to eat by themselves, especially out in restaurants. I am just fine rocking up at my favorite Sushi joint and tucking into the trays which come around on that lovely conveyor belt. The simple truth is that nobody cares about other people that much anyway. Yes, you heard that right. Nobody gives one damn about you for the most part, let alone that you're eating by yourself. If you doubt this, go and sit at the end of the bar in your local drinking establishment one evening. Watch how no one bats an eyelid while you're there. The truth is that apart from your immediate family (parents and siblings) in addition to a handful of extended family and very close friends, nobody cares what you do. They don't wish ill will upon you, they just care about themselves, and that's just fine. Let them get on with it.

A Cosmological Perspective

I say this not to make anyone feel bad or inconsequential, but to liberate you instead. It's a counterintuitive way to act. As in reality, nothing that we do in this world will be more than a fart in the wind when compared to the backdrop of cosmological time. Everyone thinks that their situation is so important. But its a paradox, your life is simultaneously the most profound (to you) but pointless occurrence (to others) when measured against what has been achieved and what is yet to come. Think of the empires that were built in the past which have now turned to dust. Cornelius Vanderbilt amassed a $215 billion shipping and railroad conglomerate in the mid-1800's (2018 inflation-adjusted figure). Although almost all of this wealth has been squandered within just three generations of miss management.

Dan Peña is a revered business mentor who's famous for turning $800 into over $450 million in the 1980's. He's a polarizing Bond villain type character who now lives in a castle in Scotland. But love him or hate him, he has some sage advice on life. When asked by his mentor Constantine Gratsos, the CEO of the Onassis Shipping company, "Mr. Peña, what would happen if I put my hand into that toilet bowl?" Somewhat confused and looking for a poetic response, Peña simply said: "Well sir, your hand would displace the water." "And what would happen when I removed it?" Mr. Gratsos replied. "Well, the water would just go back to where it was sir." "Exactly," he said. "That is life, Mr. Peña." So what are we all worrying about?

Another interesting thing to do is analyze the responses of the inhabitants of retirement homes when interviewed about their lives. There's a hauntingly familiar theme to the answers you hear, in that nobody ever states things that they regret they have done. It's always the things they didn't do. Not spending enough time with people they truly loved. Not starting that business adventure when they had the chance. Not traveling more when they were young. Not asking that one girl to marry them.

Minimalism just frees you up to actualize these things more readily without becoming bogged down in the usual minutiae. You can take more risks as you have less to lose. It allows you to focus on that one purpose driven goal you have chosen to pursue. But it takes a rewiring of your belief systems, so you might as well reassess and realign them while you still have time to do something about it. If you need some further advice on exactly how to do this, then the following chapter is the perfect place to start.

CHAPTER 12: LEARNING TO LET GO

"Minimalism is the pursuit of the essence of things,
not the appearance."

(Claudio Silvestrin)

The previous three chapters should have given you some pointers on how to effectively clear the mind of clutter, as well as take a good hard look at your current thinking patterns and belief systems. This is an important step to make; it's a crucial starting point to cultivate the right mindset for minimalism to prosper. Meditation and mindfulness practices set the table in terms of preparing you for a harmonious lifestyle. They ensure there's only space for what is truly important, and what YOU decide to fit into your thinking. If there is one other area that you want to master when it comes to minimalist living, it's this, I.e., learning to let go of things in your mind.

Severing the psychological connections to your physical possessions, as well as your negative emotional relationships, is the key to a healthy existence in this world. It has undoubtedly been the thing which has created the most peace within my life. You can't throw out that old sentimental painting or wedding gift if you do not come to terms with losing it in your mind first. I honestly feel an attachment to very few things now. It's so much more liberating when you can do this. I'm not handcuffed continuously to my possessions and now unburdened by the stress of losing them.

Many of you may be thinking that this would be too difficult for you to achieve in your current mindset. Your connection to objects in your life is just too strong. To that I would say, take it slow. Merely thinking about things in a new light forces the mind to consider a different perspective. Don't rush things, to begin with, just try to care a little less each day with regards to the menial elements of your current situation. Remember that minimalism isn't about clearing everything out, just that which is unimportant. It allows you to cherish what you do have that much more. If you are struggling to embody this feeling in your current state, then I encourage you to try the following strategy.

Cultivating an Attitude of Gratitude

One of the best ways of learning how to let go of things is to truly appreciate the possessions and relationships you do have. To genuinely feel gratitude towards them more often. To be thankful for the good times, the moments of joy we all experience throughout our day, no matter how large or small. This practice honestly changed my life when I made this small switch in my mind. I used to believe that being grateful for the sake of it was silly. I viewed it as an immature mentality. But this is only really down to the conditioning we receive as adults. It seems as though we are never truly satisfied with our lot in life. This mentality can be both a benefit and a hindrance depending on how you look at it. It can propel us forward to strive for greater achievements, but equally, ensure we feel like we are not enough as we currently are.

I can attest to this myself. When I was first setting out on my minimalism journey, my day was filled with much more stressful situations, and my problems seemed to engulf everything. So why would I be grateful for my current circumstance? Wouldn't that just be making do? After all, I had much larger goals for myself in the future. But much like goal setting and visualization, the mind doesn't work this way. The subconscious aims to serve you more of what you are feeling right now. If you are abundantly happy and grateful for what is in your present existence, then it will go to work on finding other such situations to bring your way. The mind doesn't understand the difference between joy in having a good day or winning the World Cup. If you think positively and gratefully, you will simply bring yourself more to be grateful for, and this is far easier when you cut down the clutter to only the essential.

During my college days, I had another friend who I would regularly meet up to dine with. We used to convene in the dorm canteen and pick out the dishes we wanted to eat that day. However, when we arrived at the checkout counter, the lady calculating our meals would almost always get something wrong. We would frequently have to correct her to obtain the correct total. It was obvious that she wasn't trying to cheat us. If anything she would typically undercharge us! But being good humans like we are, we would always clarify and make sure we paid the right amount.

Although, this would never fail to rile my friend. He could never understand why this lady couldn't get the total accurate in the first place. In reality, it only required an additional 10 seconds to sort out each time, but it still frustrated him to the point of consistent anger. He would often question me as to why I never let it bother me, to which I simply asked him to think about it for a moment. What would he prefer, be an A grade student with a great career path ahead of him, but have to endure a minor delay each time he paid for his lunch? Or be the lady who has to serve hundreds of annoying college kids all day? His outlook on the situation immediately changed. "You're right he claimed, what was I thinking? I'll give her a break from now on!"

While I certainly do not like to waste my own time and believe in attaining efficiency whenever and wherever possible in life. After all, this is the very base principle of the philosophy I'm laying out in this book. But I can also appreciate the bigger picture, and make sure I'm not "sweating the small stuff" to the detriment of my mindset. Being grateful for the things you do have has such a significant impact in being able to achieve this in my experience. It's important to remind yourself from time-to-time, that the modern world we enjoy, affords us a standard of living that our great-grandparents would have found staggering. I'm not suggesting to not push for your loftier goals and a better life. Just temper this with an appreciation for what you do have in the here and now, take some time to smell the roses. If you are diligently working towards a worthwhile goal, and making genuine progress towards it, then you will feel a level of unrivaled contentment and great satisfaction.

But the majority of people fall into the trap of thinking they can only be happy at some future point in time when they have achieved this goal they are aiming for. Whether this is a promotion at work, a new house or the perfect life partner. All noble things to strive for indeed. But you have to find a way to be happy with the journey, to enjoy the process as you move along the path to attainment, then the results will take care of themselves. Remember that the mind doesn't know the difference between now and this future point of success. In reality, that future point will be "in the present moment" when it arrives anyway. So you might as well enjoy yourself now!

But its all well and good me telling you this, but how do you put this mindset into practical use for yourself? One way I find works great is to note down everything for which you are grateful for now from the smallest observation to your biggest achievement. Create a list much like your top 20 goals we already covered. Such things might include you and your family being in good health, having a great circle of friends, possessing a particular skill or attribute which allows you to make a living or excel in some sporting context. I have cultivated this to a point within myself that I'm grateful for a new day now. I enjoy the sun the rain and the snow equally. It's all good and positive experiences for me, just in different weather.

I look at my goals and gratitude lists each morning when I wake, and before retiring to bed each night. You have to really feel what it's like to unconditionally appreciate these things and attach as much positive emotion to them as possible. You're subconscious is most in tune during these times, and will begin to conjure up bigger and better things for you to be grateful for down the road. Your creativity centers start to function at full throttle, and you will notice that you are making great strides towards your goals and aspirations in no time. Regardless of your current situation, you have to take responsibility for your mindset in this manner, as nobody else can do it for you.

What Will Be Will Be

I previously stated my admiration for the work of Eckhart Tolle. Much of his advice on clearing the mind, differentiating between the observer and mindless chatter, can undoubtedly produce profound effects on the person who chooses to implement this within their own lives. Perhaps the most powerful of these concepts is the notion of "dying before you die." I remember coming across this concept in my early 20's. But in truth, it was wasted on me back then. I wasn't ready to integrate the entirety or implications of this advice. It wasn't until I re-read this section of Tolle's work in my 30's, did I genuinely appreciate the extent of these words. It also struck a chord with much of the minimalist content I was now consuming. So don't be disappointed if this doesn't immediately jive with you, give it some time to stew. It's a game changer when you eventually get it.

But most of us are far to caught up with our day-to-day activities to ever really contemplate these questions. We live as though our current situation is all there is, and waste time as if we will live forever. It's often stated that a person is no more alive than when they no longer fear death. It strips away all of the neuroses which get in the way of truly living. This notion applies to whatever you are trying to achieve, whether that is creating a minimalist lifestyle, or becoming the President of the United States. Grasping this concept allows you to work for these things unhindered by self-sabotaging behavior. I'm not making any metaphysical claims to what might happen when we do leave this world. But fearing your physical death is a sure way to live a less fulfilling life while you are here. When I struggle with this, I always remind myself of the famous words of one Doris Day, that "Que Sera Sera, whatever will be will be."

The Old Zen Master

Another of my favorite ways of looking at this concept comes from the old Zen Master himself. This is actually a very famous Taoist story which has such profound significance on the human mindset once you integrate it. In fact, it dictates almost every other mode of rational and pragmatic thinking, which is crucial for minimalism to succeed as a thinking tool. It took me a number of years to appreciate this in practice. But once I did, it changed everything. If you do not know what I'm referring to, then let me explain. There are a few variations of this timeless fable, but the gist of the story goes something like this:

There once was a farmer who worked his land with the aid of a trusty horse. One day the horse bolted away, and the town folk all lamented "What bad luck that is!".

The Zen master replied, "We'll see."

Later that afternoon the horse returns, bringing with it two additional wild horses. To which the town folk cheer "How lucky that is!".

The Zen master once again replied, "We'll see."

A few days pass before the farmer allows his son to take one of the horses as a gift on his sixteenth birthday. To which to villagers cry, "How wonderful that is!"

The Zen master says, "We'll see."

It doesn't take more than a week for the young lad to be thrown off the saddle of his new companion breaking his leg in the process. All of the town folk lament, "How Awful!"

The Zen master replies, "We'll see."

The village is then visited by military officers who draft all the young men to go to war. But the boy can't fight as his leg is in a cast. Everyone states, "Oh, how lucky that is!"

The Zen master says… you've guessed it by now.

The story of the farmer and his son is now something which automatically springs to mind whenever I'm about to get rid of something or let it leave my life. It's a tendency I've trained into myself over the years. The words "We'll see" naturally pop into my head now during these instances. It immediately dissipates any feeling of panic for the perceived loss. I know that nothing is ultimately good or bad and that something positive can be gleaned from any situation. Even if its the peace of mind and mental clarity you gain from letting it go. You also train yourself to deal with any eventuality, as a by-product of this thinking, as you know that there's honestly no point in stressing about "bad" situations for more than a second.

In fact, it's an excellent practice to start seeing the opposite side of any coin you may be looking at from the outset. Start to envisage your life after you have let that certain thing go. Take the worst case scenario to its ultimate conclusion, and realize you can easily deal with this eventuality. Yes, you may feel some momentary grievance for no longer having that possession, but you'll get over it almost immediately with this mindset. So don't be held hostage to your things or the fear of letting them go. Simply utter the words "We'll see" in your mind, the next time you do decide to give something the heave-ho. You will immediately feel more balanced when you do!

CONCLUSION

"Having more and more won't solve the problem, and happiness does not lie in possessions or even relationships. The answer lies within ourselves. If we can't find peace and happiness there, it's not going to come from the outside."

(Tenzin Palmo)

I honestly couldn't put it any better than that. This quote perfectly summarizes the concept of minimalism when its done right. Any personal development process you wish to start first begins in the mind of the individual. I intentionally wrote this first book for this very reason, to give you the psychological tools which are so critical to develop, to allow you to succeed with minimalist living. You have to understand what you're up against when it comes to inherent human thinking tendencies.

The psychological factors which propel us to seek new experiences and become creative are the same traits which ensure we become bored with the status quo just as quickly. This is why we typically accumulate so much stuff; we crave the thrill of that new gadget or garment of clothing. These things excite us for a time, but once we've played with them for a while, the novelty soon wears off. We discard these items in the cupboard never to see the light of day again.

This doesn't seem to end the wealthier we become or more material possessions we accumulate. There is always a faster car to buy, and there is yet still a bigger house to purchase. This is also why you can't console the losing team's quarterback at the Super Bowl. Even though he has tens of millions of dollars in his bank account, three mansions, and the trophy wife. He's still distraught as none of this currently matters. All of those material possessions are par for the course, its what he's become accustomed to. He wanted the one thing he doesn't yet have, I.e., the ring around his finger and the accolades of winning the biggest sporting event in the country.

No matter how rich you become, you can only eat one meal at a time, regardless of how expensive it is. You can only drive one car at a time. Even the guy who tests drives Ferrari's for a living gets bored at some point. These things have diminishing returns the higher the price tag goes. This is why I say that minimalism is not a mindset for going without. But rather a quality over quantity measure instead. We have to become satisfied with what we do have. If you want something new, then replace the old. Don't continually add to your current collection.

"Minimalism is a mindset for life, not just for Christmas."

(Me)

All of the advice contained within the previous chapters is designed to help you do just that, to aid in streamlining your life. But in truth, it runs even deeper than that. Why are we trying to cut down the unneeded stress, worry, and clutter in the first place? Because ultimately, we want to be happy. But as I've already stated, happiness is elusive for most of us. Its a place everyone hopes to arrive at, at some future point in time. However, the momentary feeling of joy you experience when you do achieve something you're striving for is always fleeting. It's immediately replaced and upgraded by a new goal or a new ideal to aim towards. Then the cognitive dissonance kicks in once more, and unhappiness returns as the default state to your being.

Henry David Thoreau suggests the way to combat this is to "Make yourself rich, by making your wants few." This is the typical minimalist mantra and is indeed one way to achieve a more harmonious mindset. What he is really saying is not want for nothing, but intentionally focus on only that which is important to you. In this sense, much of minimalism has to do with finding your true purpose in life. Then just doing that. Even if you haven't worked out what this is for you yet. Becoming a minimalist allows you much more time and space to discover it, rather than filling your days with endless distractions.

But you can only do this when you are free of your things. It's really about attachment. A toy is just a toy until its given to a child; then it becomes the property of the kid. It becomes their all em-compassing world for a time. Of course, they lose interest in it before long, but they still consider it theirs. No other sibling is allowed to play with it either. It's not until a parent explains the notion of sharing is the child able to let go in some sense. As adults, we simply need to re-learn to do the same. We too have toys, just the larger and more expensive kind. We have the technological gadgets and gizmos, all the way up to our prized automobiles. But as we've seen already, many times these things own us, not the other way around!

This is a radical re-contextualization for most people at first. It's difficult to dismiss the message we've been soaking in from society all of these years. Some are so ingrained, like excessive consumerism for instance, that they are almost impossible to resist without some significant fightback.

Hopefully, this is where I step in. I'm here to tell you to live your life by design instead. Don't plod along on autopilot not making the necessary adjustments to your thinking. There's going to be some resistance in your mind, to begin with, in addition to those around you. The other crabs will start to drag you back down into the bucket. If so, then go and re-read the chapter on improving your relationships and inner circle.

But ultimately it's about freedom. I believe that all humans yearn for this on a deep level. In reality, the more stuff you have, the less free you are. You need to bring more order to the chaos of life, as Jordan Peterson would put it. Embrace simplicity and strip things down to only the most essential, rewarding and fulfilling. The only way to honestly do this, in my opinion, is to cultivate minimalist living as your default mindset. If you can, then the world is your oyster. So do not read this and just nod your head at the principles. Start to put them into practice yourself. It will be well worth the effort I promise you.

I started this book with a story about the mother and daughter at Thanksgiving to help you alter your perspective a little, and I'll finish with another one. It's also a favorite short story of mine regarding the fisherman and the businessman. One day a successful city guy took a trip to the beach, and after sitting down, he noticed a fisherman rowing his small boat back towards the shore carrying his catch. Impressed the businessman asked the fellow, "How long does it take you to catch those fish?" The fisherman replied, "Oh, not that long." "So why don't you stay out longer to increase your haul?" Replied the businessman. "Because this is plenty to feed my family" the fisherman replied. "So what do you do for the rest of the day?" asked the businessman. "I go out to sea early in the morning, so I can get back to play with my kids at lunchtime. I then take an afternoon nap with my wife before having beers and playing guitar with friends at the local bar".

The businessman then offers some advice. "I have an MBA from a top school and could help you become more successful. Why don't you spend more time at sea and increase your catch? Then you will make more money, can buy a larger boat and catch even more fish. Then you can afford multiple boats and hire additional people. Before long you can start your own canned fish company and move to the city and manage the entire operation." "And after that?" the fisherman replied. "Well, then you can sell the company and become rich!" "And after that?" The fisherman replied. "After that, you can finally retire and move to a little fishing village, wake up early each morning, catch some fish, go back and play with the kids, take a nice nap with the wife, and by the time the evening comes around you can go and drink, dance and sing with your buddies!" The businessman states.

Somewhat puzzled the fisherman replied, "Isn't that what I'm doing now?"

All the best

Jason

P.s. I just want to thank you for purchasing this book personally. If you happened to enjoy the content than I'd love to hear your feedback. I would very much appreciate if you could leave a review after reading. Comments on how these concepts may have helped you are both interesting for me to read, as well as aiding others in finding this information!

Printed in the USA
CPSIA information can be obtained
at www.ICGtesting.com
LVHW020259060224
770950LV00008B/131